BASKETBALL

About the Authors

Pat Summitt
Head Coach
University of Tennessee, Knoxville

One of the most respected taskmasters in the game of basketball, Pat Head Summitt of the University of Tennessee (UT) can make a claim that no other coach—male or female—can make. She has led the U.S.A. to an Olympic gold medal as a coach (1984) and an Olympic silver medal as a player (1976) and her UT Lady Vols to two NCAA Championships (1987 and 1989).

Summitt, who has compiled a 412–113 record and taken her Tennessee team to the Final Four ten times during her 16-year career, has been compared to a combination of Dean Smith of North Carolina and Bobby Knight of Indiana basketball fame. In addition, she has been honored as Coach of the Year numerous times.

Summitt began her odyssey when, as an eager 22-year old, she was handed the head coaching reins at Tennessee. She has fashioned her coaching philosophy behind one solid statement: "Offense sells tickets; defense wins games."

Pat Summitt played basketball and volleyball at the University of Tennessee at Martin, earning her B.S. degree in 1974 in Physical Education. In 1976, she completed her master's degree at the University of Tennessee, Knoxville, while teaching physical education classes, coaching the women's basketball team, and training for a spot on the first U.S.A. team in the women's Olympic basketball competition.

Debby Jennings
Assistant Athletic Director for Media
University of Tennessee, Knoxville

For a dozen years, Debby Jennings has chronicled the accomplishments of Coach Pat Summitt's Tennessee Lady Vol teams. Jennings also has been on board for six U.S. Olympic Festivals, the 1983 and 1989 World University Games, the 1984 Olympic Games, and the 1987 Pan American Games. While representing the United States Olympic Committee on these junkets, she was often responsible for basketball media coverage.

Over the years, she has been decorated a number of times by the College Sports Information Directors of America for her media guides. Jennings graduated from the University of Tennessee, Knoxville, in 1977 with a B.S. in Journalism.

BASKETBALL

Pat Head Summitt

**Associate Athletic Director and Women's Basketball Coach,
University of Tennessee–Knoxville**

Debby Jennings

**Assistant Athletic Director/Media Relations, University
of Tennessee–Knoxville**

Wm. C. Brown Publishers

Book Team

Editor *Chris Rogers*
Developmental Editor *Cindy Kuhrasch*
Production Coordinator *Peggy Selle*

 Wm. C. Brown Publishers

President *G. Franklin Lewis*
Vice President, Publisher *George Wm. Bergquist*
Vice President, Publisher *Thomas E. Doran*
Vice President, Operations and Production *Beverly Kolz*
National Sales Manager *Virginia S. Moffat*
Advertising Manager *Ann M. Knepper*
Marketing Manager *Kathy Law Laube*
Production Editorial Manager *Colleen A. Yonda*
Production Editorial Manager *Julie A. Kennedy*
Publishing Services Manager *Karen J. Slaght*
Manager of Visuals and Design *Faye M. Schilling*

Cover photo by Bob Coyle

Cover design by Jeanne Marie Regan

Consulting Editor
Physical Education
Aileene Lockhart
Texas Women's University

Sport and Fitness Series
Evaluation Materials Editor
Jane A. Mott
Texas Women's University

Library of Congress Catalog Card Number: 89–82335

ISBN 0–697–07889–2

Printed in the United States of America by Wm. C. Brown Publishers, 2460 Kerper Boulevard, Dubuque, IA 52001

10   9   8   7   6   5   4   3   2   1

I would like to dedicate this book to my families—my parents Richard and Hazel Head, my husband R. B. Summitt, and all the coaches, players, and administrative support staff who make up the Lady Vol basketball family at the University of Tennessee, Knox-ville.

Contents

Rules of the Game 83

7

Preface

Basketball: Fundamentals and Team Play is an introductory look at the game that encompasses basic terms, concepts, skills, and strategies. This book covers all aspects of basketball, beginning with the fundamentals and then elaborating on team play.

The game of basketball has enjoyed tremendous growth during the last 25 years. The National Basketball Association (NBA) has expanded . . . Title IX ushered in a burgeoning of women's intercollegiate basketball teams . . . Junior Olympics, AAU competition, and boy's and girl's All-Star Camps all over the country make the game a 12-month sport . . . women's basketball was introduced in the Olympic Games in 1976 . . . the National Collegiate Athletic Association (NCAA), the largest governing body of intercollegiate athletics in the United States for men and women, realizes millions of dollars in revenues from the men's Final Four . . . and the list goes on and on.

Basketball is essentially a game for everyone.[1] Solitary figures are often seen playing "the final buzzer" on playgrounds all over the country. Free throws have been practiced relentlessly in gyms, parks, and at the hoop in the driveway at home. "Winners stay and losers sit" games go on in marathon fashion.

No matter what the level of play or the aspirations of the player, basketball is a game of building blocks. This book considers all of the components of the game that lead to the development of a complete player. The book is assembled in the same way a coach typically approaches the season. Starting with the basics of conditioning and weight training, footwork, shooting, passing, offensive and defensive patterns, drills, strategy, and rules of the game, this book can be used for all levels of teaching and coaching.

I would like to thank the women who have been University of Tennessee Lady Vols, the members of the five international teams I coached from 1977 to 1984, and numerous high school and college coaches who have influenced me in the teaching and coaching profession. In particular, I would like to thank my Olympic coaches Billie Moore and Sue Gunter, my Olympic assistants Kay Yow and Nancy Darsch, and my University of Tennessee assistants Mickie DeMoss and Holly Warlick.

Special thanks to William "Bill" Wall, Executive Director of U.S.A. Basketball for the opportunities and support he has given me through the years.

---

1. To facilitate the use of inclusive language, male pronouns are used in even-numbered chapters and female pronouns are used in odd-numbered chapters when we refer to "the player."

I would like to thank the reviewers for their helpful comments and suggestions: John C. Carter (The Citadel College), Dr. Harry Hitchcock (Auburn University), Dr. Buck Jones (University of Tennessee, Knoxville), Angela Lumpkin (North Carolina State University), Jenny Moshak (University of Tennessee, Knoxville), Robert D. Symons (University of North Florida), and Karen R. Toburen (University of Wisconsin–LaCrosse).

The following symbols are used in the diagrams throughout this text:

●   =   Ball

——————▶   =   Player movement

– – – – – –▶   =   Ball movement (pass)

——————┤   =   Screen

〰〰〰▶   =   Dribble

History of the Game

1

Colleges and universities are institutions of higher learning where students generally are challenged and encouraged to voice an opinion or to make a mark on society. With that in mind, it is almost fitting that a group of bored and discontented college students were the reason the game of basketball was invented.

In 1891, the mandatory winter indoor physical activity classes at the School for Christian Workers (now Springfield College in Massachusetts) were boring the students. The dean of the Department of Physical Training, Dr. Luther Gulick, presented a young second-year graduate student with the unenviable task of developing an activity game that would interest the students.

For two weeks James Naismith's activity games were unsuccessful. Then, in late December, he introduced a game, complete with thirteen rules, called "basketball." Perhaps the most lucid explanation of what happened comes from basketball rules expert Dr. Edward S. Steitz in his *Illustrated Basketball Rules.* According to Steitz (currently a well-known figure around the Springfield College campus himself), a custodian was unable to come up with the 15-by-15-inch boxes needed to serve as goals.[1] Instead, "Pop" Stebbins could only offer old half-bushel peach baskets to Naismith. The baskets were nailed into the lowest railing of the balconies at either end of the gymnasim. The height from the floor to the basket happened to be 10 feet, and almost 100 years later, the distance has not changed.

Naismith's original Code of Rules has withstood the test of time practically unchanged. Some of the rules were modified and adapted in the early years, but the amount of foresight Naismith had when he developed the game of basketball was amazing. Some of his original rules concerned the following: two officials, the passing of the ball, dribbling, fouls, how to score, 5-second count on the inbounds pass, two halves plus halftime, how to win the game, and a tiebreaker rule.

The new game caught on quickly. As a matter of record, the first women's basketball game was played at Smith College just three months after Naismith invented it. In fact, Naismith met his future wife while watching a women's game of pick-up basketball in Springfield in 1892.

Because the School for Christian Workers (Springfield College) trained students who were studying to go into service with the Young Men's Christian Association (YMCA) all over the world, the game of basketball spread from continent to continent in short order. YMCAs, colleges, and universities were

1. Steitz, Edward S., *Illustrated Basketball Rules,* 1st ed. (New York: Doubleday, 1976), pp. 1–5.

staging intercollegiate competition within months after the game's introduction. Forty-five years after the first game in Massachusetts, men's basketball became a contest in the Olympic Games in Berlin in 1936, with its founder, Dr. Naismith, then 75 years old, in attendance.

The rest is history. Basketball is popular worldwide as a team sport played by millions and a spectator sport viewed by billions. From the NCAA Final Four to the NBA Championships, from the Olympic Games to high school and youth leagues, blacktop and hardwood enthusiasts have favorite teams, players, and moves.

The game has remained rock-steady throughout the years. Modifications—such as the 24-, 30-, or 45-second shot clock, dunks, three-point goals, and extra officials—have added to the excitement for both the spectator and player. Essentially, the collegiate court is 50 feet wide and 94 feet long with an 18-inch cylindrical hoop, basket, or goal suspended on a 4-by-6-foot fiberglass, glass, or wood backboard raised 10 feet above the court. High school courts are generally 10 feet shorter, but the other dimensions apply.

Points are earned when one of the five players on the offensive team (the team with the ball) scores a one-point unguarded shot called a free throw, a two-point shot called a field goal, or a three-point goal (shot outside a specially marked area 19 feet 9 inches from the basket in the college and high school game) against the defense (the team without the ball).

The defense protects its team's basket and, without fouling, attempts to prevent the offense from scoring. A foul is called when a player violates a rule or gains a favorable advantage over the opposition illegally. The ball is moved up and down the floor by passing or dribbling, and the action stops only when an official blows the whistle or the official horn signals the stop of play.

The five players on each team play both offense and defense. Generally, teams consist of two guards, typically shorter players who set the offense and handle the ball a great deal; a forward, who looks to shoot and penetrate to the basket; and two taller players called posts or centers, who can score close to the basket and rebound shots that do not score as baskets. Perhaps the idea of calling two players "posts" instead of using the traditional line-up terminology of "guard, guard, center, forward, forward" seems a little confusing. It really isn't at all. In the two-post line-up, one of the posts is really a power forward, whereas the other is the traditional center. Today, with bigger, stronger, and taller players in both men's and women's basketball, it is more common to go with a two-post line-up.

The team that scores the most points after two 20-minute halves in college basketball is the winner. Therefore, possession of the ball is the only way to score and ultimately to win. Most coaches hope to achieve a balance between their offensive unit's ability to score and their defensive unit's ability to take the ball away.

Millions of spectators jam arenas all over the country to view the game. On December 9, 1987, 24,563 fans were shoehorned into the Thompson-Boling Arena at the University of Tennessee–Knoxville to watch the then number two-ranked

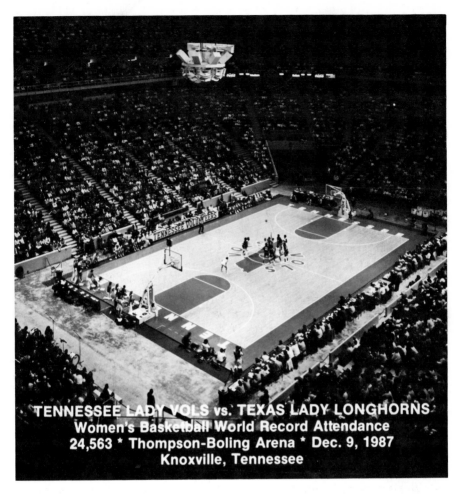

Figure 1.1
The University of Tennessee hosts the largest crowd ever to see a women's basketball game.

University of Texas–Austin defeat the number one-ranked University of Tennessee in a world-record attendance for a women's basketball game. Typically, on winter nights from UCLA to Syracuse, Georgetown to Kentucky, Indiana to Tennessee, the fans are packed to the rafters and the action is hot.

Dr. Naismith would be proud of the countless minutes of enjoyment his winter physical activity has brought to the coaches, players, and spectators on every level all over the world for almost 100 years.

Conditioning

2

Coaches have come a long way in realizing the importance of conditioning to sport-specific activities. Basketball games have been won in the final minutes by teams whose players were in superior condition. Basketball players cannot get physically fit by playing alone, however, for basketball in and of itself does not develop all the aspects of strength and fitness that the athletes need to perform to their maximum level of ability.

The skills and conditioning necessary for participation in basketball are different from the skills and conditioning required for other athletic activities; therefore, conditioning, like coaching, has become a specialized field of study and expertise. For improved basketball fitness, the areas of flexibility, strength, and muscular and cardiorespiratory endurance should be considered as elements of training by an athlete or an aspiring coach.

Flexibility

Flexibility refers to the capability of a joint to move through its range of motion. Joint motion is limited primarily by the joint capsule, ligaments, tendons, and muscles. These soft tissues can be stretched to increase flexibility, and improved flexibility can enhance performance. A flexible joint requires less energy to move and can move further through its range. Greater flexibility can help prevent injuries by allowing joints to absorb more shock and muscles to respond to outside stimuli more quickly.

Stretching is an integral aspect of the conditioning program and should be performed both before and after activity. Prior to stretching, you should warm-up with some walking or light jogging for approximately 4 minutes to raise the muscle temperature. Stretching after exercise can help reduce muscle soreness. Stretching is done in a slow, static fashion until a mild tension is felt in the muscle. Hold this stretch for 30 seconds, then move slightly further through the range of motion until a mild tension is again felt and hold for another 30 seconds. *Do not bounce* or stretch to the point of pain. Bouncing can lead to injury. Your breathing should be slow and controlled. Do not hold your breath while stretching.

The following stretches should be done before and after playing basketball:

1. *Lower back stretch*—Lying on your back, reach behind your knee and pull your knee to your chest while keeping the other leg straight. Curl your upper back slightly until you can almost touch your chin to your knee. Hold for 30 seconds, then switch legs. Repeat two to three times (Fig. 2.1).

Figure 2.1
Lower-back stretch.

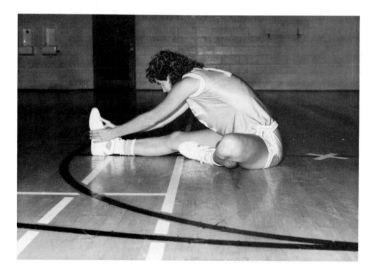

Figure 2.2
Hamstring stretch.

2. *Hamstring stretch*—Sit on the ground with one leg extended out straight and the other bent so that the sole of that foot touches your straight leg. Stretch down to the straight leg, reaching to touch your toes. Hold for 30 seconds, then switch legs; repeat two to three times (Fig. 2.2).
3. *Gluteus (buttocks) stretch*—Sit on the ground with your left leg straight. Place your right leg bent over the straight knee (foot flat on the ground) so that your right ankle is on the outside of your left knee. Put your left elbow

Figure 2.3
Gluteus stretch.

Figure 2.4
Groin stretch.

on the *outside* of the bent knee and push on your leg. Twist your upper body in the opposite direction of the bent leg. Place your free hand on the ground (after you twist) to balance yourself. Hold for 30 seconds, then switch legs; repeat two to three times (Fig. 2.3).

4. *Groin stretch*—While in a sitting position, place the soles of your feet together, drawing your heels as close to your body as possible. Grasp your ankles and gently push on the inside of your knees with your elbows. Push your knees towards the floor while bending slightly at the waist and pulling your forehead toward your toes. Hold for 30 seconds; repeat two to three times (Fig. 2.4).

Figure 2.5
Thigh/knee stretch.

Figure 2.6
Calf stretch.

5. *Thigh/knee stretch*—While standing, hold the top of your *right* foot with your *left* hand and gently pull your foot upward so that your heel touches your right buttock muscle. Keep your back straight. The knee bends at a natural angle when you hold your foot with the opposite hand. Hold for 30 seconds, then switch legs; repeat two to three times (Fig. 2.5). This stretch can also be performed while lying on your side instead of standing. In that position, the athlete can concentrate on pulling the ankle to the buttocks while also extending at the hip.

6. *Calf stretch*—Stand facing the wall with your heels placed flat on the floor. (The distance from the wall will be determined by the current flexibility of each individual. A more flexible individual will stand farther from the wall.) Place your hands on the wall and lean forward as if you were performing a push-up. Keep your right leg straight, hold for 30 seconds, then slightly bend your knee and again hold for 30 seconds. Switch legs; repeat exercise two to three times. Remember that the heel of your straight leg needs to remain on the floor (Fig. 2.6).

Figure 2.7
Ankle rotations.

Figure 2.8
Triceps stretch.

7. *Ankle rotations*—While standing or sitting, rotate each ankle in a circle (first clockwise, then counterclockwise) ten times each (Fig. 2.7).
8. *Triceps/rotator cuff stretch*—With arms over head, hold the elbow of one side with the opposite hand. Gently pull the elbow behind your head. Hold for 30 seconds, then switch arms; repeat two to three times (Fig. 2.8).
9. *Front of shoulder/rotator cuff stretch*—Stand facing the wall and grasp it with your hand at shoulder level. Look over your opposite shoulder. Keep the shoulder close to the wall while you slowly turn your head and chest away. Hold for 30 seconds, then switch arms; repeat two to three times (Fig. 2.9).
10. *Back of shoulder/triceps stretch*—Bring arm across chest. With your opposite hand, gently pull elbow across chest and toward opposite shoulder. Hold for 30 seconds, then switch arms; repeat two to three times (Fig. 2.10).

Figure 2.9
Front of shoulder stretch.

Figure 2.10
Back of shoulder stretch.

Running Programs

For any athlete, fatigue hinders one's best performance. Even low levels of fatigue have negative effects on the athlete's total performance. Fatigue not only decreases performance but it may also leave the player more susceptible to injury. Cardiovascular fitness is the most important component of a basketball conditioning program.

Basketball uses a combination of *aerobic* ("with oxygen") and *anaerobic* ("without oxygen") energy systems. Running, which is a rhythmic, large-muscle activity, is a good cardiovascular conditioning activity for both of these types of energy systems. A year-round running program for basketball can be divided into four time frames: (1) summer, (2) preseason, (3) season, and (4) postseason.

Summer Phase

Summer running programs are used to establish a distance endurance base. This is accomplished with continuous training, which, as the name implies, involves on-going activity without rest. Two types of continuous training—high-intensity or continuous activity of moderate duration, and long slow distance (LSD)—can be used to increase a player's endurance level.

High-intensity continuous activity is executed at work intensities expressed in terms of 80–85% of the player's maximum heart rate (HR max). The athlete runs at this pace for 2 to 3 miles. To determine an individual's maximum heart rate, use the following formula:

$$220 - \text{Person's age} = \text{HR max.}$$

For example, a 20-year-old player would run at a high-intensity continuous pace regulated by a heart rate of 160 to 170 beats per minute (b/m).

$$220 - 20 \text{ years old} = 200 \text{ HR max,}$$
$$80\text{–}85\% \text{ of } 200 = 160\text{–}170 \text{ b/m.}$$

To find your heart rate (pulse), place your index and middle fingers next to the larynx on your throat. Feel the same side of your neck as the hand you are using. Feel for the heart beats or carotid pulse. Count the number of beats for 15 seconds (the first beat should be counted as zero) and multiply by four. This will give you the beats per minute.

With LSD training, the athlete performs at 60–80% of his HR max. Distance, rather than speed, is the main objective; therefore, the athlete runs 3 to 5 miles. A coach must remember that it is best to gradually build up to the distance. Many players are discouraged with running programs because they tend to burn out as a result of the unreasonable distances they are asked to complete at the beginning. The following is an example of one week of a summer running program after the players have progressed through initial shorter and slower distances.

Monday—LSD, 4 miles at 70% HR max
Tuesday—Rest
Wednesday—High intensity, 3 miles at 80–85% HR max
Thursday—LSD, 4 miles at 75% HR max
Friday—Rest
Saturday—LSD, 4 miles at 60% HR max
Sunday—Alternate activity (biking, swimming, rowing)

Preseason Phase

Once a good distance base has been established by means of the summer running program, the preseason running program can be geared towards increasing the basketball player's cardiovascular fitness for competition. This is achieved by using an interval running program three days per week on alternating days for six to eight weeks. Interval running involves short periods of running alternated with short periods of rest or light activity.

A combination of short and long sprints make up the interval running workout. Whether short sprints (20, 50, or 100 meters) or long sprints (200, 300, or 400 meters) are used, the total distance should be a mile to a mile and one-quarter for short sprints and a mile to a mile and three-quarters for long sprints. To allow for metabolic and cardiovascular recovery, rest time should be on a one-to-two ratio. In other words, if the sprint takes 30 seconds to run, the rest time will be 60 seconds.

Long sprints may be done one day per week. Guards' and forwards' times for 400 meters range between 85–90 seconds and centers' times between 88–95 seconds. The 200 meter times for guards and forwards range from 30–32 seconds, whereas centers are clocked at 32–34 seconds.

Short sprints may be done two days per week. Guards and forwards should run 2 to 4 seconds faster than centers in each of these sprints.

Again, a percentage of the athlete's HR max can be used to determine an adequate work rate. A high-intensity work interval should be run at 95% of the athlete's HR max, and a moderate-intensity work interval should be run at a rate between 85–95% of the individual's HR max. The length of rest can also be determined by the athlete's heart rate. A pulse of 120 beats per minute should be obtained before beginning the next set.

Season Phase

The third stage of the conditioning program, the season phase, is designed to maintain the cardiovascular fitness gains that were developed during the preseason running program. This can be accomplished with interval running one day a week in addition to the team practices. Depending on the game schedule and conditioning achieved in practice, running may be done only once a week or not at all. A running workout should be completed at least two days prior to game day so that the leg muscles have ample time to rest before competition.

Postseason Phase

Finally, the postseason running program should be designed to give athletes a mental and physical break from conditioning and basketball while allowing them to maintain the conditioning improvements they have gained. Variety is the key to achieving this goal. Taking part in a cardiovascular activity such as running, swimming, or biking three days per week for 30 minutes a day at 60 to 80% of their HR max will help athletes to maintain their cardiovascular fitness level while the diverse exercises will help decrease boredom and the chance of burnout.

Weight Training

Only recently have basketball coaches begun to incorporate weight training or resistance exercises into their total conditioning programs. In this age of sport specificity, it is important to structure the weight-training program in such a way as to enhance a basketball player's performance. Weight training has been proven to increase speed, strength, power, and endurance, all important components of basketball.

There are three types of resistance exercises:

1. Isometrics involve a fixed speed and a fixed resistance. There is muscle contraction but no actual muscle shortening or lengthening and no joint motion. An example is pushing against a wall.

2. Isotonic exercises utilize variable speed with a fixed resistance throughout a joint's range of motion. For example, exercises using free weights or Universal and Nautilus machines are isotonic.
3. Isokinetic exercises entail a fixed speed with variable resistance throughout the joint's range of motion. An example is working out on Orthotron and Cybex machines.

Regardless of whether one trains using isometric, isotonic, or isokinetic exercises, there are four general principles that should be followed in order to benefit from resistance training.

1. *Overload.* The training program should provide a progressive heavy overload of the specific muscle groups that are to be strengthened.
2. *Large to Small Muscles.* Exercise large muscle groups before smaller ones. This will delay fatigue.
3. *Specificity/Variety.* Train the muscle groups that are used in the sport of basketball. Make the training as interesting as possible. One way of achieving this is to alternate between free weights and machines.
4. *Rest.* Allow adequate recovery of the muscles between individual exercises and between exercise periods. This principle will also help retard fatigue and allow the muscle to adapt to weight training with the least amount of soreness.

Although strength gains can be achieved by using any of the three types of resistance exercises, isotonic exercises will be given primary consideration. Isotonic exercises allow for strength gain through the joint's entire range of motion, incorporate balance with the use of free weights, and utilize the specificity principle for basketball.

Isotonic exercises use a combination of concentric and eccentric muscle contractions to perform the activity. With a concentric muscular contraction, the muscle shortens as it develops tension and overcomes the resistance. When the muscle contracts eccentrically, the external resistance overcomes the active muscle and the muscle lengthens while developing tension.

Before developing a program, each individual must determine his repetitions maximum (RM). One RM is the maximum weight that can be lifted correctly one time. A percentage of that 1RM is then calculated to perform the exercise. For example, if 1RM = 100 pounds, 60% of 1RM = 60 pounds, and that is the actual working weight. A repetition (rep) is the number of times a given weight is lifted. A set refers to a group of repetitions (e.g., 1 set = 10 repetitions).

Basketball weight-training exercises may include bench presses, squats, leg curls, leg extensions, latissimus pull downs, heel raises, upright rowing, flys, wrist curls, wrist extensions, sit-ups, obliques, deltoid raises, bicep curls, and tricep extensions. The following are examples of basketball weight-training workouts.

Preseason Workout to Increase Strength

60–65% of 1RM—1 set/12 reps
75% of 1RM—1 set/8 reps
85% of 1RM—1 set/5 to 6 reps
60–65% of 1RM—1 set/until fatigue
Sit-ups (crunches)—3 sets/15 reps holding for 5 seconds
Obliques—3 sets/25 reps

To do sit-ups (crunches), lie on your back with your legs straight. Place your hands across your chest (for more resistance, place your hands behind your head but do not interlace your fingers). Slowly curl your head and shoulders up to the point where your shoulder blades just come off the ground. At the same time rotate your hips backwards so that your lower back touches the floor (you are trying to eliminate the curve in the lower back). Hold this position for five seconds, then return to the starting position.

To perform obliques, sit on a bench with a light bar across your shoulders and wrap your straight arms across the bar. As you keep your legs, hips, and head pointed straight ahead, twist (rotate) your trunk to the right and to the left in a slow, controlled motion. Twisting to the right and then to the left equals one repetition.

In-Season Workout to Maintain Strength Gains

80–90% of 1RM—1 set/1 to 12 reps
65%–75% of 1RM—1 set/6 to 8 reps
Sit-ups (crunches)—3 sets/15 reps holding for 5 seconds
Obliques—3 set/25 reps

Weight-Training Tips

- Stretch before and after training.
- Use slow, controlled movements.
- Breathe normally (do not hold your breath).
- Always have a spotter when doing free weights.
- Go through the full range of motion.

Re-evaluate your 1RM approximately every four weeks. During an isotonic training program, rest time between sets of each lift (machine or free weights) should be kept to a minimum to overload the muscle. The rest time between the different exercises should be approximately 1–1½ minutes. To save time, the athlete can alternate activities (for example, arms, legs, arms, legs, and so on). The rest period between workouts should be at least 24 hours to allow full muscle recovery. These exercises should be done two or three times a week during the off-season, every other day during the preseason, and two times a week during the competitive season.

Before implementing a weight-training program, consult a conditioning book or a coach or athletic trainer with expertise in this area.

References

Arnheim, D. D. 1985. *Modern principles of athletic training.* St. Louis: Times Mirror/Mosby College Publishers, 112–148.

Brooks, G. A., and T. D. Fahey. 1985. *Exercise physiology: Human bioenergetics and its application.* New York: MacMillan, 412–414, 432–441.

Fleck, S. J., and W. J. Kraemer. 1988. "Resistance training: Basic principles." *The Physician and Sports Medicine* 16: 160–171.

Fleck, S. J., and W. J. Kraemer. 1988. "Resistance training: Physiological responses and adaptations." *The Physician and Sports Medicine* 16: 63–74, 108–124.

Katch, C. I., and W. D. McArdle. 1988. *Nutrition, weight control, and exercise.* Philadelphia: Lea & Febiger, 193–239.

Kraemer, W. J., and S. J. Fleck. 1988. "Resistance training: Exercise prescription." *The Physician and Sports Medicine* 16: 69–81.

Lamb, D. R. 1984. *Physiology of exercise: Responses and adaptations.* New York: MacMillan, 272–292, 295–309.

Fundamentals

3

Unlike football, every player at each position in basketball handles the ball, dribbles it, passes it, shoots it, and rebounds it. Thus, no matter what the level of play, good fundamentals and ball handling are essential.

Footwork

Balance is a key fundamental ability in the game of basketball. To achieve and maintain good body balance, an individual must develop good footwork. This allows a player to start, stop, jump, change directions, pivot, and play the game under control.

Stops

There are two basic stops that a player should learn to use: the jump stop and the two-step stop.

The jump stop is the technique used when a player lands on both feet at the same time. To be in a good triple-threat position, the shooting foot should be slightly forward.

The two-step stop is the technique used when a player lands first on one foot and then follows closely with the other foot, landing slightly forward or in the triple-threat position.

In both stops, the feet should be approximately shoulder width apart and the weight should be on the balls of the feet. This position allows the player to use either foot as the pivot foot. The knees should be slightly bent, the head up, and the back fairly straight.

Pivots

The pivot is a technique used to change direction by keeping one foot in constant contact with the floor while turning the body in a circular pattern. There are two types of pivots: the forward pivot and the reverse pivot.

The forward pivot occurs when a player keeps one foot stationary, with the weight on the balls of the foot, and then steps forward or toward the opponent.

The reverse pivot is simply the opposite. A player keeps one foot in contact with the floor and steps back or pivots away from the opponent.

Figure 3.1
Triple-threat position.

Figure 3.2
Placement of hands for passing.

Triple-Threat Position

The triple-threat position, often referred to as the ready position, is a position by offensive players in which they assume a balanced stance that will allow them to pass, shoot, or dribble the basketball. In this stance the player should be balanced with the knees bent and the body square to the basket. The ball is held in a shooting position to allow the player to be threatening offensively. The feet are positioned in a staggered stance approximately shoulder width apart with the shooting foot (or foot on the side of the dominant hand) positioned slightly forward (Fig. 3.1).

Individual Offensive Skills

Passing

One option out of the triple-threat position is the pass. Although there are various effective passes in the game—from plain to fancy to impossible—four basic passes will be covered in this section (Fig. 3.2).

Figure 3.3
Chest pass.

Figure 3.4
Chest pass follow-through.

As passing skills are developed, players may improve their passing by using fake passes. The offensive player may use a fake with the ball to make the defense react in a certain direction. For example, the offensive player could fake an overhead pass and when the defense reacts by putting her hands up, the offense could quickly use a bounce pass. The passer should eventually be taught to pass without looking at the target to avoid being predictable to the defense.

Chest Pass

One of the most fundamental passes taught in basketball is the chest pass. The ball is supported at chest level primarily by the fingertips. The thumbs should be positioned behind the ball with the hands and fingertips spread out toward the sides. The elbows should be positioned close to the body. With the feet in a triple-threat position, the weight should be on the back foot and rotated forward as the player steps into the pass, extends the arms, and rotates the thumbs downward.

To increase speed and distance, emphasis should be placed on shifting the body weight quickly and snapping the wrists as the thumbs are rotated toward the floor. The passer should focus on the target (Figs. 3.3 and 3.4).

Figure 3.5
Overhead pass—hands position.

Overhead Pass

The two-hand overhead pass is quickly becoming one of the most popular passes in today's game. Why? Because the overhead pass can be executed with speed and accuracy over a long distance. It may be used to make an outlet pass to begin the fast break or as a skip pass to swing the ball from one side of the floor to the other (Fig. 3.5).

The ball should be held just above the head with the hands and fingers spread on each side. The palm of each hand should be cupped as the ball is firmly supported by the fingertips. The elbows are turned to the outside of the body. As the player is positioned with feet in a staggered stance, the weight should be shifted from the rear to the forward foot as the ball moves from the top of the head forward. The ball is released out in front of the head as the fingers and wrist snap forward toward the receiver (Figs. 3.6 and 3.7).

Bounce Pass

The bounce pass has become a popular pass. It is often used on the fast break or in a half-court offense by perimeter players to get the ball inside to post players.

A two-hand or one-hand bounce pass may be successfully executed. In using either, the passer places the hands or hand behind the ball, extends the arms, and releases the ball in a downward fashion. The ball should hit the floor at two-thirds of the distance to the receiver. With proper wrist rotation and forward spin, the ball should rise just above the receiver's waistline. Bounce passes can be used to deliver the ball under and away from the hands of the defense (Figs. 3.8 and 3.9).

Figure 3.6
Overhead pass.

Figure 3.7
Overhead pass continuation.

Figure 3.8
Bounce pass.

Figure 3.9
Bounce pass follow-through.

Figure 3.10
Baseball pass.

Figure 3.11
Shooting form.

Baseball Pass

When a team employs the fast break, the baseball pass is frequently used to begin the break or pass the ball ahead of the defense. This one-hand pass allows the passer to throw the ball a long distance, much like the outfielder throwing the baseball to home plate.

The baseball pass begins with a staggered stance and the ball held primarily in one hand (the throwing hand). The ball is supported initially by the nonpassing hand. It is then guided by both hands just behind the shoulder of the throwing side as the weight is shifted backward. On the throw, the passing hand extends in a forward and upward motion. The ball is released as the arm straightens (Fig. 3.10).

Figure 3.12
Shooting form.

Figure 3.13
Shooting form.

Shooting

Often shooting is what players enjoy most about the game, and thus it is the most practiced skill in basketball. Let's face it, when you walk into a gym and pick up the ball, the first thing you do is shoot at the basket. Great shooters are not born. Their skills are developed by technique, concentration, and repetition.

The perimeter players—guards and forwards—are usually referred to as long-range shooters. Some perimeter players may be able to shoot from three-point range, but most attempt to shoot from 17 feet or closer. Post players will most likely attempt shots near the basket or in the free throw lane area.

High-percentage perimeter shooters are those who shoot 50% or better, whereas post players may shoot above 60%. An average team shooting percentage will range between 46–48%. Of course, 50% or better would be considered an above-average percentage for a team.

Although the primary objective is to shoot the ball so that it enters the basket and falls through the bottom of the net, different techniques and angles may be used to accomplish this objective. Shots may be taken from in front of the rim, at a 45-degree angle (side), from the baseline, or above the rim. When shooting from in front or on the baseline, the target or focus should be the rim (Figs. 3.11, 3.12, and 3.13). A shot taken at a 45-degree angle may be aimed either at the rim or at the backboard. A shot in which the ball hits the backboard before entering the basket is referred to as a bank shot. The bank shot is considered to be

Figure 3.14
Lay-up—the take-off.

Figure 3.15
Lay-up—the basket.

a high-percentage shot for post players or other players who take shots close to the basket. The shot taken from above the rim is called the dunk. This is a technique used when the offensive player shoots the ball down through the basket.

For a player to become a high-percentage shooter, proper shooting techniques should be learned and repeated. Repetition will help to develop concentration and confidence, which are important aspects of becoming a consistent shooter. Three basic shots essential for today's fundamentally skilled player include the lay-up, the jump shot, and the free throw.

Lay-Up

One of the oldest and most fundamental shots in the game is the lay-up. Because it is a shot taken close to the basket, it is considered to be a high-percentage scoring opportunity while the offensive player dribbles or drives to the basket.

The lay-up is a shot that should be taken at a 45-degree angle to the basket or backboard. When approaching from the right side, the shooter should plant the left foot while raising the right foot and extending the body in an upward

Figure 3.16
Jump shot sequence 1.

Figure 3.17
Jump shot sequence 2.

motion toward the basket. The ball should be held by the right hand, slightly supported by the left, and lifted toward the backboard as the body extends upward toward the goal.

The backboard is the target used in this particular shot. The ball should hit to the right of the basket near the top of the painted square. Different angles and approaches may be used for the lay-up. The left-handed lay-up should be executed by reversing the approach as just described (Figs. 3.14 and 3.15).

Jump Shot

The jump shot is one of today's most advanced shooting techniques. The jump shot is properly performed when the player shoots under control, pushes up into the air, and shoots the ball over the defense and toward the basket.

The ball should be held by the shooting hand and supported by the non-shooting hand. The hand is cupped or positioned so that the ball does not rest in the palm. The ball is primarily controlled by the fingertips. The elbow needs to be under the ball in line with the foot on the shooting-hand side. As the player stops in a bent-knee position, she jumps, extending the legs, elbow, and arm in one fluid motion. The ball is released near or at the peak of the jump. The shooting hand follows through toward the target with a snap of the wrist (Figs. 3.16, 3.17, and 3.18).

Figure 3.18
Jump shot sequence 3.

Figure 3.19
Free throw position.

Free Throw

The free throw is a shot taken from behind the free throw line and is considered a high-percentage shot because no defense is present to contest it. However, it is usually one of the most tense and critical shots, as it often can result in winning and losing a close game (Fig. 3.19).

The shooter should establish a ready position with the knees bent and arm and hand properly positioned as in the basic jump-shot technique. On the release of the shot, the arms and hands extend, as do the legs, with proper follow-through of the shooting hand.

Concentration and repetition are important for developing consistency. Each shot should be the same in stance, bounce, extension, and follow-through. The best free throw shooters appear to be the ones with the most consistent approach.

Figure 3.20
Control dribble.

Dribbling

The dribble is a technique used to advance the ball while repeatedly bouncing it to the floor with one hand. The two basic types of dribbles are the control dribble and the speed dribble. Advanced players will utilize the hesitation, crossover, and reverse dribbles. A combination of these fundamentals using change of speed and change of direction can be an effective way for a skilled offensive player to gain an advantage over the defense.

Control Dribble

The control dribble allows the offensive player to dribble the ball in a low fashion while protecting it from the defender. The feet should be spread apart, the weight on the balls of the feet, the knees bent, the back fairly straight, and the head up.

The ball should be dribbled by one hand, controlled by the fingertips, and positioned away from the defense to protect it. The ball should be bounced so that it rebounds off the floor between knee and waist level (Fig. 3.20).

Figure 3.21
Reverse dribble—1.

Figure 3.22
Reverse dribble—2.

Speed Dribble

To allow the offensive player to quickly advance the ball up or down the court, the speed dribble is used. The ball handler uses more of a running motion as the ball is pushed out in front of the body at waist to mid-chest level.

Hesitation Dribble

The hesitation or change-of-speed dribble is a combination of the control and speed dribbles. The offensive player can change speeds to fake the defensive player and then accelerate by the defender. When used effectively, the offensive player can gain an advantage or beat the defense with the hesitation dribble.

Crossover Dribble

The crossover move may be used in a control or speed dribble to protect the ball from the defender, to move by the defender, or to change directions. The crossover dribble takes place by switching or bouncing the ball from one hand to another. It is referred to as the crossover because the ball crosses in front of the body from the left to right hand or vice versa.

Figure 3.23
Reverse dribble—3.

Figure 3.24
Reverse dribble—4.

Reverse Dribble

In the reverse dribble, the ball handler changes directions by planting the inside foot or foot closest to the defender, pivoting quickly, and turning the back toward the defensive player. As the ball handler reverse pivots, the ball changes hands and the body changes direction (Figs. 3.21, 3.22, 3.23, and 3.24).

One-on-One Skills

Individual offensive skills should be taught and drilled to enhance a player's scoring ability. The player with the ball must be able to create, through her own ability or skill, ways to score against the defense.

Jab Step

The jab step is a technique used by the offensive player with the ball to fake the defense and create a scoring opportunity. This maneuver begins with the offensive player facing the basket in a triple-threat position. The offensive player steps or jabs at the defense with the front foot, keeping the pivot foot stationary. If the defense takes the fake by stepping back, the offensive player quickly returns to a balanced or triple-threat stance and shoots. (This is also referred to as the jab and shoot.)

If the defense does not take the fake on the jab, the offensive player steps by the defense. This is called the jab and go. The pivot foot must remain on the floor until the dribble starts. In this move, as in all one-on-one moves, the first step is the most important. It must be executed quickly and precisely in order to beat the defense.

Crossover

The crossover move is the one technique in which the player has the ball in the triple-threat position and then steps across and by the defense with her front foot. For protection, the ball should be moved to the outside hand farthest away from the defender. The dribble begins before the player picks up the pivot foot.

Shot Fake

Shot fakes may also be used to gain an advantage over the defense. The offensive player fakes a shot to the basket and quickly responds to the defense. If the defense does not come out to defend the shot, the offense shoots the ball. This is referred to as the shot fake and shoot. If the defense reacts by raising up, the offensive player steps to the side and by the defense. This is the shot fake and drive.

Two-Player Skills

Team play is vital to success in basketball. One-on-one moves may be flashy and draw "oohhhs and aahhhs" from the crowd, but they will not often win games. Two-player and three-player concepts allow a coach to take small groups of individuals to work on specific techniques within a team concept. Teamwork, timing, and execution of fundamentals are the key ingredients in these skills.

Cuts

Cutting is an offensive maneuver used by a player without the ball to cut or break in an open lane to the ball or the basket. The cutting maneuver is usually made by a player away from the ball who is looking to receive the ball in a scoring position.

V-Cut

The V-cut is the technique most commonly used by an offensive player to get open to receive the ball. A good example is when a wing player cuts to get open to receive the ball from the point guard. The player may begin on the wing, break toward the basket, stop, pivot, and cut back out to the wing for the ball. Change of speed, change of direction, and straight-line cuts aid the offense to get free of the defense, receive the ball, and square up to the basket.

Backdoor Cut

The backdoor cut is the V-cut in reverse. The player may start in close to the basket, break out for the pass, stop, pivot, and cut backdoor to the basket for the pass.

Give-and-Go

The give-and-go is a two-player offensive technique in which the player with the ball passes to an open player and cuts to the basket or an open area on the court. Change of speed, change of direction, and sharp cuts make the give-and-go most effective.

Screen and Roll

The screen and roll, or pick and roll, is used to screen the defense and get an open shot. The player without the ball moves to one side of the defender on the ball and executes a jump stop. The screener should be stationary with her feet spread slightly more than shoulder width apart and arms placed across her chest to discourage illegal use of the hands. The offensive player must step foot-to-foot with her teammate as she begins to dribble and run her defensive player into the screen with her head up. As the player with the ball steps closely by the screener, the screener uses a reverse pivot and rolls toward the basket. The player with the ball watches the defense and determines whether to shoot, drive, or pass the ball to the roller (teammate who screened), depending on the action of the defense (Figs. 3.25, 3.26, 3.27, and 3.28).

Three-Player Skills

Two-player concepts can be effective for a variety of scoring options, but other techniques require the addition of another player. Three-player concepts generally utilize a passer, a screener, and a cutter. Action off the ball is important in these concepts because it has a great effect on the timing of a play.

Screens

Screens off the ball or picks off the ball have become popular offensive techniques in today's game. The player with the ball must be able to see the players without the ball. One player away from the ball screens for another player without the ball to free that player for a pass and potential scoring opportunity. The screener must set up in a stationary position to block off the defense from the offensive player using the screen to get open. The player or cutter to the ball must step foot-to-foot to the screen or in a manner to run the defense into the screen (Figs. 3.29, 3.30, and 3.31).

Figure 3.25
Screen and roll—1.

Figure 3.26
Screen and roll—2.

Figure 3.27
Screen and roll—3.

Figure 3.28
Screen and roll—4.

Figure 3.29
Screen off the ball.

Figure 3.30
Screen off the ball—continuation.

Figure 3.31
Screen off the ball—continuation.

Splitting the Post

Also referred to as the scissors cut, splitting the post is another three-player concept used within the halfcourt offense. This is used most commonly with two guards and a center or with a guard, forward, and post or center. The center sets up at the high post position with her back to the basket. The player with the ball passes to the high post or post player. The passer then make a cut either off or closely (foot-to-foot) by the post player with the ball to the outside of the court. The nonpasser makes the second cut off the post player to the opposite side of the court. The post player must watch the defense and determine whether to pass to the first or second cutter, pivot and look to shoot, or drive to the basket. The basic idea is to find the open player for the best scoring opportunity.

Rebounding

One of my high school coaches, Mike Jarreau, had a favorite saying: "Offense sells tickets, defense wins games." After several years of coaching, I have added a third line to the saying: "Rebounds win championships."

Rebounding is a key fundamental because it can greatly influence the game at both ends of the court. It is a skill that can be developed to a great extent by repetition of rebounding techniques and improvement in anticipation. Rebounding is much more than jumping ability—it is the ability to get position.

Figure 3.32
Offensive rebounding A.

Figure 3.33
Offensive rebounding B.

Offensive Rebounding

In each offense, players should be taught their specific area of responsibility in rebounding. Most coaches send three or four players to the boards and one back as the safety. The weakside board is a high-percentage rebounding area. Because the defense is usually positioned between the offensive player and the boards, it is necessary for the offense to anticipate the shot and react by getting by or in front of the defense. Offensive players should avoid the box-out position by the defense or attempt to keep moving and get around the defense.

Two specific formations that may be taught are the triangle-and-one and the semicircle. In the triangle-and-one formation, three players rebound in a triangle position under the basket, with one player going to the free throw line and reacting to the ballside. The fifth player is the safety. When four players are sent to the boards, they should form a semicircle under the basket with one player back as a safety (Figs. 3.32 and 3.33).

Defensive Rebounding

The term most frequently used in reference to rebounding on the defensive end is "box out." The defense may use a front pivot or a reverse pivot to box out a player. Regardless of which pivot it uses to achieve box-out position to screen the player off the boards, contact should be made in the following manner: the player boxing out should position her rear into the player behind her. The feet should be spread wide apart to form a solid base and the knees bent slightly, the elbows should be out and the hands up and open to the ball (Figs. 3.34, 3.35, and 3.36).

Figure 3.34
Defensive rebounding position.

Figure 3.35
Defensive rebounding—continuation.

Once position has been established to prevent the offense from getting the ball, the defense should quickly withdraw from contact and go for possession of the ball (Fig. 3.37).

In a player-to-player defense, each player is responsible for preventing the person she is guarding from rebounding the ball. In a zone defense, players are responsible for boxing out the offensive player in a specific area. Regardless of the defense being played, each person must anticipate the shot and react by physically positioning her body between an offensive player and the basket.

Free Throw Rebounding

The inside players, or two defensive players closest to the basket, should be aware of stepping in to the lane and making contact with the offense in the same basic box-out stance as previously explained. A defensive player should be designated to step in to the lane on the shot and box out the shooter.

The offensive players line up next to the defensive players, and on the release of the shot, they try to step quickly toward the goal and by the defense. A reverse pivot may be used by the offense rather than the box out to try to gain an advantage or allow the offense to get around the defense.

Figure 3.36
Defensive rebounding—"box out."

Figure 3.37
Defensive rebounding—going to the boards.

Team Offense

Teaching an offense can be compared to a cook using a recipe. Ideas may be borrowed but put together with different styles, variations, and ingredients.

Offensive sets may vary from a 1-3-1, 1-2-2, 2-2-1, or 1-4 set, depending on the strength of the personnel. If a team has a strong perimeter game, a single post offense may be preferred, whereas a post-oriented team may be best suited for a double post or high-low post game. Offenses may be designed for one-on-one play, two-player concepts, or three-player concepts.

Building a Team Offense

The following checklist can serve as a guide for building a team offense:

( ) Personnel
( ) Shot selection
( ) Reading the defense
( ) Spacing
( ) Player movement
( ) Ball movement
( ) Timing
( ) Rebounding
( ) Offensive signals
( ) Number system

Before selecting an offense or offensive style, coaches should have their own philosophy, but it is important that they have some flexibility depending on their personnel. They might prefer a running game, but if they do not have the players to run, they should adapt their offense to best suit their personnel. The best ball handlers should handle the ball, the best shooters should take a high percentage of the shots, and the rebounders should be in position to rebound.

While presenting the offense to the team, shot selection should be covered. High-percentage shots will usually be reflected in the team's overall shooting percentage. The coaches and players should identify which shots are preferred by individual players. Players should attempt shots within their scoring range and avoid forcing shots.

If players can learn to "read the defense" or recognize the opponent's individual team defense, they can together become a smarter or more effective offensive team. Players need to recognize whether the opponents are in a player-to-player or zone defense. Are they in an even front or an odd front zone? How are they playing on the ball defense? Are they forcing the ball to the sideline or to the middle?

Reading post defense is an important responsibility of the perimeter players. Are they playing in front, behind, or to the side of the post player? Reading the defense helps to determine the best passing angles, best types of passes to make, and most effective ball and player movement.

Spacing of players on offense is important to ensure good floor balance. This provides an inside and outside offensive threat with good rebounding position. Proper spacing also allows the offense to spread out the defense. This prevents one defensive player from guarding two offensive players.

Players without the ball should be aware of the importance of movement without the ball. They should remain active, acting as a decoy or entertaining their defensive player to prevent that player from helping out.

Ball movement is just as important as player movement. Quick passes and penetration can put pressure on the defense or force the defense to react. Quick reversal passes can be effective in attacking the helpside defense, or defense away from the ball.

Timing is essential to running any offense effectively. Timing includes player movement and ball movement. Players work together in sequence. They should know when to cut, pass, screen, or dribble in relation to the ball and their teammates. Timing should be discussed and practiced with each offense taught. An example is a cutter moving to the ball when the ball is in position to be passed, or an offensive player waiting for a teammate to set a screen on the ball before dribbling.

Rebounding positions should be covered so that all players know what area to cover for offensive rebounds. Second shots can provide the offense with easy, high-percentage scoring opportunities. A designated player or safety will be responsible for protecting fast break opportunities if the opponents rebound a missed shot.

Offenses may be verbally signaled, or hand signals may be preferred. To avoid being predictable, some teams will predetermine specific offenses by which side of the floor the entry pass is made or which type of pass is used to begin the offense. Regardless, the coach should make certain that all players know what offense is being run at all times if more than one offense is being utilized.

In teaching an offense, it is important to establish a system that enables players to understand and follow their designated assignments. Most coaches prefer to use a number system, which would apply to the offenses explained in this text.

#1—Point guard
#2—Swing guard, or shooting guard (wing)
#3—Forward (wing)
#4—High post, or power forward
#5—Low post, or center

The #1, #2, and #3 players are considered the perimeter players, whereas #4 and #5 are the inside or post players.

Offensive Patterns

The offenses discussed in this text—the single post, double post, and flex—are designed as "continuity offenses." Such offenses allow players more than one scoring option in an organized and continuous pattern that flows and does not have to be reset.

Single Post

A single post offense may be most effective for a team with strong perimeter players and only one true post player. The single post offense illustrated in this text should be a simple offense to teach, learn, and execute.

The guards should set in a two guard front with the two wing players at their respective wing positions. The post player will have the option of setting up at either a high or low post.

Four options or patterns may be used in this particular offense:

1. If the post player sets up high and receives the ball, the split-the-post option will be run;
2. If the post sets up high and the guard passes to a wing or a forward, the give-and-go and screen-away options will be executed;
3. When the post sets up at the low post, the ball may be passed directly to the post player for a one-on-one option; or,
4. The guard may pass to the forward and the post will step out for the screen-on-the-ball option.

All perimeter players should be aware of where the post player sets up initially. The #1 player will be the designated safety, or person to first defend the opponent's basket should a change of possession occur.

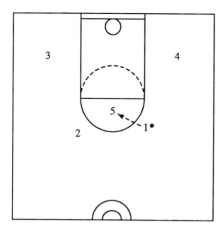

Figure 4.1
Split-the-post option (high post).
#1 passes to #5 and becomes the first cutter.

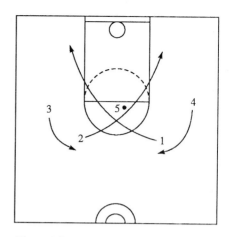

Figure 4.2
Split-the-post option—continuity.
#2, the nonpassing guard, will be the second cutter.
#4 will replace #1.
#3 will replace #2.
#5 looks to pass to #1 or #2 or pivots and looks for a shot or drive.

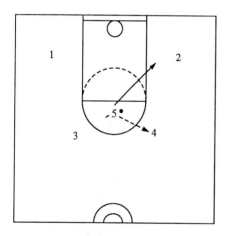

Figure 4.3
Split-the-post option—continuity.
If #5 does not take a shot, the ball may be passed to any perimeter player. To continue the offense, #5 may remain at the high post or cut to the low post for a give and go option.

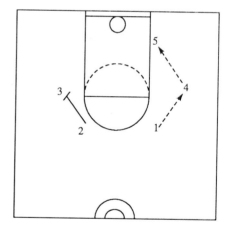

Figure 4.4
One-on-one option (low post).
#5 begins at low post.
#1 passes to #4.
#4 passes inside for one-on-one.
#2 has option to screen for #3.

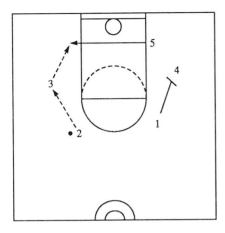

Figure 4.5
One-on-one option (opposite low post).
#2 passes to #3.
#5 cuts to low post (ballside).
#3 passes inside to #5 for one-on-one.
#1 has option to screen for #4.

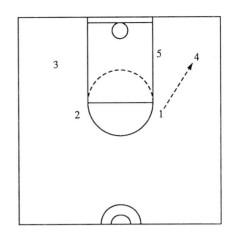

Figure 4.6
Screen-on-the-ball option (low post).
#1 will pass to #4 to begin the offense.

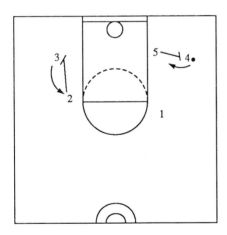

Figure 4.7
Screen-on-the-ball option—continuity.
#5 will screen for #4 and roll to the basket.
#2 will screen for #3 to entertain helpside defense.
#1 will be a safety.

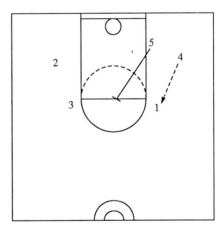

Figure 4.8
Screen-on-the-ball option—continuity.
If a shot is not taken, #4 may pass to #1, and the offense continues with #5 setting up at the high post.

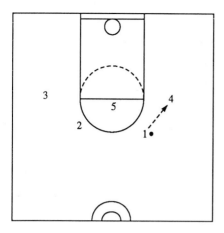

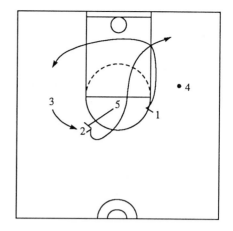

Figure 4.9
Give-and-go and screen-away options (high post).
#1 begins offense with a pass to #4.

Figure 4.10
Give-and-go and screen-away options—continuity.
#1 runs a give-and-go to the basket and clears.
#5 screens for #2, who cuts to the basket and clears.
#5 pivots to receive the ball from #4 and looks to score.
#3 replaces #2.
#4 replaces #1.
Offense may continue.

Double Post

The double post offense is best suited for a team with two or more good post players and a strong inside game. This particular offense is designed to get the ball inside whenever possible. Various options may be used within this 1-2-2 set to allow for one-on-one play, two-player concepts, and three-player concepts.

General Rules

Perimeter

1. #1 player dribbles the ball slightly to one side of the floor to begin the offense.
2. #2 and #3 (wing players) get open at the free throw line extended by using a V-cut or setting behind the post (stack set).
3. Perimeter players become an offensive threat by getting open within their scoring range, looking to score or pass to the post.
4. Wing players should hold the ball if the ballside post screens away to see if the post cutting to the ball is open.
5. When the wing entry is denied, a dribble entry should be used in which the point replaces the wing and the wing (intended receiver) replaces the point.
6. Perimeter players must be able to read the post defense, execute screens off the ball, and screen on the ball.
7. #1 player is designated the safety.

Post

1. Post players set up initially at the medium post area and face the defense to force a defensive decision on positioning.
2. Post players have a 2-second count and screen rule—they post for 2 seconds and must screen away unless they have the defense pinned for the open pass.
3. Post players must duck in or flash the lane when the ball is in the middle of the floor or at the top of the key.
4. The weakside post player must face the ball to anticipate a screen, shot, or skip pass.

All players must be aware of spacing and keep the offense spread in order to spread the defense. Players away from the ball must move off the ball or "entertain the defense" simultaneously with the post screens. The double post offense has the following options:

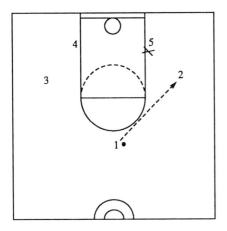

Figure 4.11
Pass and stay.
#1 passes to #2; #1 and #2 players read the post defense.
#1 stays up top for a return pass from #2 and straight-on pass to post.

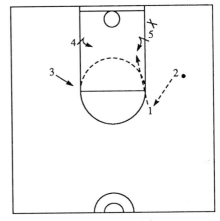

Figure 4.12
Pass and stay—continuity.
#2 passes to #1.
#5 and #4 duck in lane.
#1 looks for #5 and #4 posting.
#3 works to get open for a possible reverse pass.

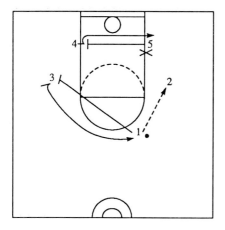

Figure 4.13
Pass and screen away.
#1 passes to #2.
#2 looks for a possible pass to #5.
#5 screens away for #4 (2-second count).
#1 screens away for #3.
#2 keeps the ball to see if #4 is open off the screen.

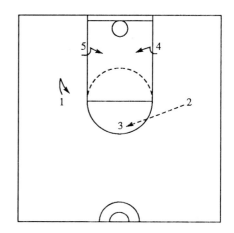

Figure 4.14
Pass and screen away—continuity.
#2 passes to #3.
#5 and #4 duck in lane.
#1 gets open for a reversal pass.

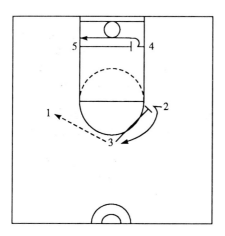

Figure 4.15
Pass and screen away—continuity.
#3 passes to #1.
#5 screens away for #4.
#3 screens away for #2.

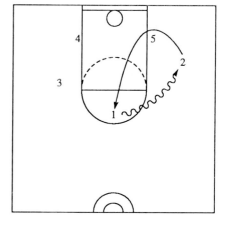

Figure 4.16
Screen on the ball (dribble entry).
#1 uses the dribble entry when the wing is denied or a point signals the wing to clear.
#2 cuts backdoor and up the middle to replace #1.

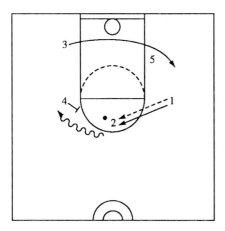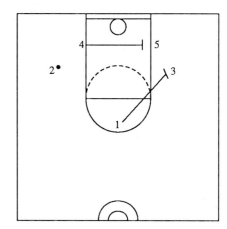

Figure 4.17
Screen on the ball—continuity.
#1 passes to #2.
#4 sets a screen at the elbow for #2 and rolls to the basket.
#3 clears the baseline to replace #1 as #1 replaces #2.
#5 anticipates the shot.

Figure 4.18
Continuity into 1-2-2.
If #2 keeps the ball, #4 posts (two count) and screens for #5 as #1 screens away for #3.

Flex Offense

A very popular offense for teams at all levels of play in recent years has been the flex offense. This offense is used against player-to-player (man-to-man) defenses. If a team does not have a true post player, the flex might be a good offense to employ. Although it provides posting options, all players must be able to play all positions and pass effectively.

The flex is a motion offense with structure and one that teaches discipline and ball control. Normally, the flex offense is popular with teams, as it provides equal scoring opportunities for all players.

In this book the flex offense is somewhat different from the original flex offense because only two entry options will be covered, but the basic continuity will be explained in detail.

General Rules

1. Entry passes must be made to the high post or ballside wing.
2. Be patient and take only high-percentage shots (lay-up or jump shots).
3. The first look is for the lay-up.
4. Elbow cutters look for the jump shot.
5. This is a passing offense; penetration is used to balance offense or improve passing angles.

6. Chest or overhead passes should be made from elbow to elbow or free throw line across.
7. Fake passes can be extremely effective in this offense.
8. Set good screens, wait on screens, and use screens effectively.
9. Use good cuts, change of speed, and change of direction.
10. The touch-and-go option can be effective against a sagging or switching defense.
11. The #1 player is the designated safety unless that person is the lay-up shooter; if so, the passer is the safety.
12. Keep the offense spread out and read the defense.

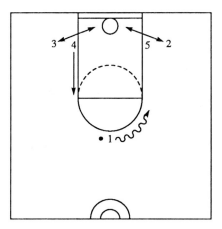

Figure 4.19
Basic set for flex offense—post entry.
All players face #1.
#1 dribbles to the right of the key as #4 cuts up to the elbow for the entry pass.
#5 positions for a screen on the pass.
#3 stays wide.
#2 sets up the defense for the cut off the screen set by #5.

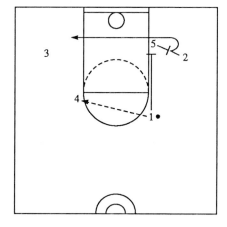

Figure 4.20
Options off the entry pass.
#2 cuts off the front or rear screen set by #5 for the lay-up.
#1 screens down for #5.
#5 cuts to the elbow for a jump shot.
#1 reverse pivots for post-up and then cuts out to the wing.

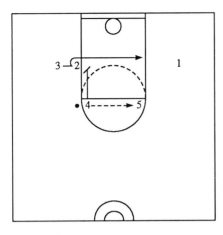

Figure 4.21
Entry pass—continuity.
#4 passes across to #5.
#2 sets a front or rear screen for #3.
#3 cuts off the screen set by #2.
#4 screens down for #2.
#2 cuts to the elbow.
#4 reverse pivots, posts up, and cuts to the wing.

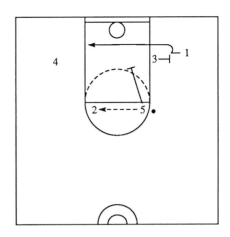

Figure 4.22
Options off the entry pass—continuity.
#5 passes across to #2.
#3 sets a front or rear screen for #1.
#1 cuts off the screen set by #3.
#5 screens down for #3.
#3 cuts to the elbow.
#5 reverse pivots, posts up, and cuts to the wing.

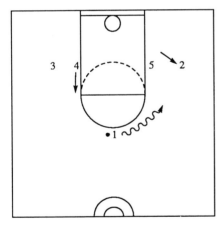

Figure 4.23
Basic set for flex offense—wing entry.
#1 dribbles to the right of the key as #2 cuts to the wing and #4 cuts to the elbow.

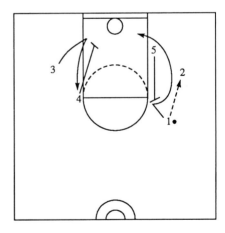

Figure 4.24
Options off the entry pass.
#1 passes to #2.
#5 sets up a screen for #1.
#1 cuts off the screen to the basket.
#4 screens down for #3.
#3 cuts off the screen to the elbow.
#4 reverse pivots, posts up, and cuts to the wing.

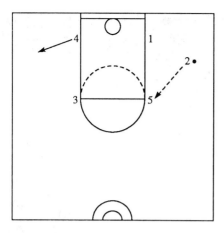

Figure 4.25
Options off the entry pass—continuity.
#2 passes to #5.
#5 looks for #1 and #4 posting.

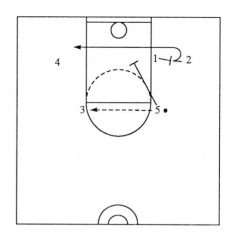

Figure 4.26
Options off the entry pass—continuity.
#5 passes across to #3.
#1 sets a front or rear screen for #2.
#2 cuts off the screen set by #1.
#5 screens down for #1.
#1 cuts to the elbow.
#5 reverse pivots and posts up.

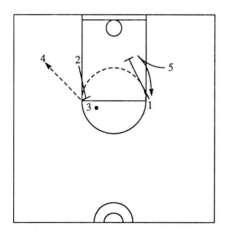

Figure 4.27
Elbow-to-wing option.
#3 passes to #4.
#2 sets up a screen for #3.
#1 sets a screen down for #5.
#5 cuts to the elbow.
#1 reverse pivots (cuts to the wing) and
posts up.

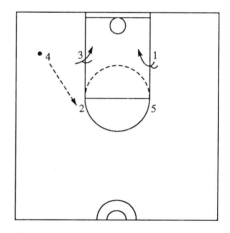

Figure 4.28
Elbow-to-wing option—continuity.
#4 passes to #2.
#2 looks for #1 and #3 posting.

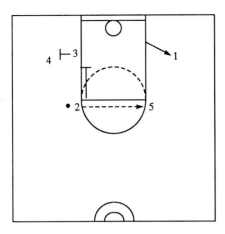

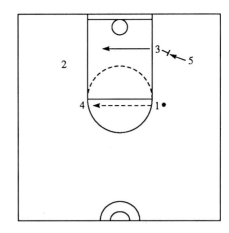

Figure 4.29
Elbow-to-wing option—continuity.
#2 passes across to #5 as #1 cuts to the wing.
#3 sets a front or rear screen for #4.
#2 screens down for #3.
#3 cuts to the elbow.
#2 reverse pivots and posts up.

Figure 4.30
Touch-and-go option.
#1 passes to #4.
#3 sets a front or rear screen for #5.
#5 touches #3 and calls "go" option.
#3 cuts across the lane.
The continuity is the same as the regular flex.

The touch-and-go is an option to use against a sagging or switching defense. The player who is cutting off the screen may touch the screener and call "go" to signal the screener to become the cutter, and the cutter will replace or take the position of the screener.

Zone Offense

Opponents frequently use a zone defense to encourage the offense to take perimeter shots. It is important for the offense to have a balanced attack against a zone defense. The type of personnel a team has on its roster will have an important effect on which specific patterns to use. Regardless of personnel, a few basic guidelines may be used in all types of zone attacks.

General Guidelines

1. Mount a balanced attack to provide an inside and outside scoring threat.
2. Attack zones with passes, penetration, screens, and player movement.
3. Recognize the seams, gaps, or open areas in the zone.
4. Create overload situations to gain a numerical advantage.
5. Skip passes or ball reversal may be used to force the defense to shift.

The offense that follows is a 2-3 alignment, which may be used against an even or odd front-zone defense (1-2-2, 2-3, and so on). This offense is designed to attack defenses with the guidelines just mentioned. In particular, this offense provides opportunities to attack the baseline area. It will be referred to as the *baseline offense*.

Once the patterns are learned, penetration will help to create better passing angles and scoring opportunities. Fake passes and skip passes may be used most effectively.

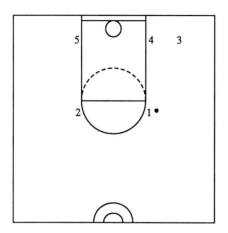

Figure 4.31
2-3 zone offense—basic alignment.

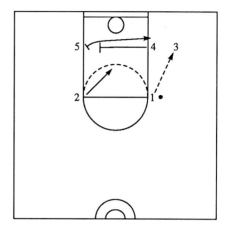

Figure 4.32
First-pass option.
#1 passes to #3.
#4 screens for #5.
#2 will cut in to the high post and replace.
#3 looks for #5 or #2 or passes out to #1.

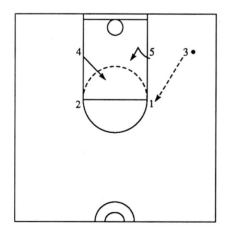

Figure 4.33
First-pass option—continuity.
#3 passes to #1.
#5 will duck in and post.
#4 will cut or flash to the ball.
#2 will create a passing lane for reversal.

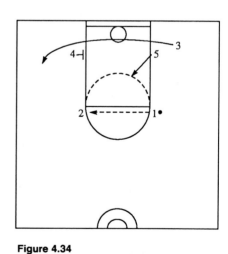

Figure 4.34
First-pass reversal.
#1 passes to #2.
#4 sets a screen for #3 and ducks in the lane.
#5 will cut or flash to the ball.
#2 looks for #3, #5, or #4.
#1 will create a passing lane for reversal.

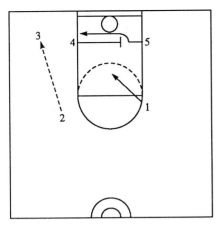

Figure 4.35
First-pass reversal—continuity.
#2 passes to #3.
#4 screens for #5.
#1 will cut in to the high post and replace.
#3 looks for #5 or #1 or passes out to #2.

Press Offense

A press offense is the offensive attack used against a full court pressing defense. Team members must train against pressure so that they do not hit the panic button if and when a team presses them in a game. It will be important that the offensive players make good passes, meet their passes, make good cuts off the ball, read the defense, and make quick and smart decisions.

Against a player-to-player press, the simplest offense is to get the ball to the best ball handler and clear out all of the offensive players in the backcourt. Usually this causes the defensive players to go away from the ball to fall into their zone or to follow their assigned offensive players downcourt. The ball handler may then dribble the ball against only one defensive player.

It may be necessary for a player to screen for the intended receiver in order for the inbounds pass to be made against denial or pressure defense. The press breaker illustrated (Fig. 4.36) is designed to attack primarily a zone defense. The intent is to get the ball inbounds quickly and provide the following options: (a) advancing the ball in the middle, (b) advancing it up the sideline, (c) reversing the ball behind the press, or (d) passing it long. To determine the best option, the player with the ball should face the defense and see the whole court. Players should try to move on each pass to stay ahead of the ball.

At the end of the press offense, a team should look for the high-percentage shot or set its offense, if necessary.

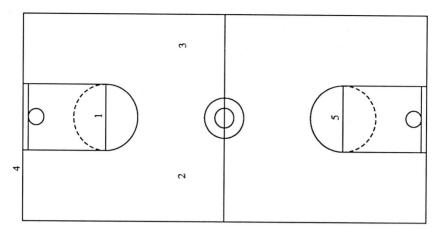

Figure 4.36
Press offense—basic alignment.

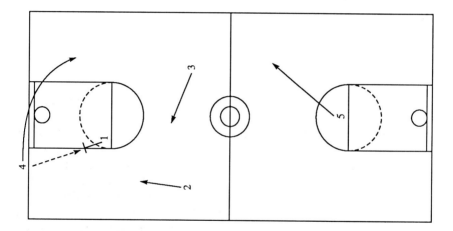

Figure 4.37
Options on the press offense.
Player #1 has the option to penetrate the middle.
If #1 does not penetrate up the middle, #2 looks to cut into an open area on the sideline.
#3 cuts to the open area in the middle for a possible pass.
#5 cuts to an open area for a possible baseball pass.
#4 cuts opposite #1 for possible reversal.

Fast Break

Athletes today are taller and stronger, run faster, and jump higher. As a result, the game of basketball has changed significantly. The overall speed at which the game is played has increased, creating an exciting spectator game. Game scores in the 1960s might have averaged in the 70-points-per-game range as most teams chose to play "set-it-up and work-it-in basketball." Other teams, up until the introduction of the shot clock, would get a comfortable lead, slow down the game,

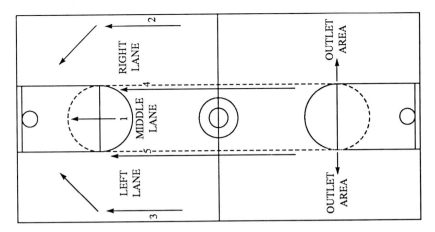

Figure 4.38
Numbered fast-break alignment.
#1 fills the middle.
#2 fills the right lane.
#3 fills the left lane.
#4 fills lane space between #1 and #2.
#5 fills the middle lane to ballside high post.

and "stall" until time ran out and victory was assured. Many teams today score more than 100 points in 40 minutes of play. How? It's called transition basketball.

The fast break has become an integral part of play for high-scoring offensive teams. The quick transition from defense to offense to gain a numerical advantage (three-on-two or two-one-one) and shoot a high-percentage shot can be entertaining and challenging. Team members should be able to handle the ball at a fast tempo, maintain good body control, and be in excellent condition.

To have a disciplined and organized break, it is necessary to know when to run and how to run. The fast break may be employed when the defense gets a steal, secures a rebound, or gains possession after a made basket. When to run may also depend on the team's personnel and the coach's philosophy.

To run successfully, a team should be organized. Most coaches will tell you that they want their teams to run under control. The numbered break allows a team to run in an organized fashion with players assigned to fill one of the five designated areas shown in Figure 4.38.

The #1 player, or point guard, will be responsible for getting open in the outlet area and dribbling the ball to the middle or cutting to the middle area and receiving a pass from a teammate to begin the fast break. The #1 player is the primary ball handler and decision maker in this particular break. The #1 player is the "quarterback" on the break, deciding whether to pass ahead, take the shot or the drive, or set a halfcourt offense. It is this player's responsibility to determine if the offense has a numerical advantage or a high-percentage shot.

The #2 and #3 players are the wing players, who are responsible for filling the outside lanes. The #2 player will fill the right lane and the #3 player the left lane, and both will sprint to get ahead of the ball. In order to spread the defense, it is important that they run wide until they reach the free throw line extended area. At this point, a diagonal cut toward the basket may enhance a high-percentage scoring opportunity such as a lay-up or bank shot.

The #4 player will be the designated trailer and will fill the lane space between the #1 and #2 players. The #4 player will cut or fill to the ballside low post position. The #5 player will fill the middle lane to the ballside high post area.

As the fast break progresses, #1 advances the ball down the court by using a speed dribble or pass to either wing player. The perimeter players should look for a lay-up, bank shot, open shot, or drive to the basket.

If the perimeter players do not take a shot off the primary break, they look to score off the post players or secondary options as diagramed.

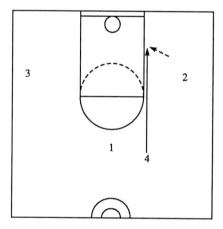

Figure 4.39
Fast break secondary option.
#2 may pass to trailer #4 for the lay-up.

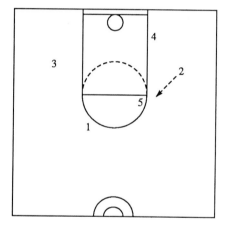

Figure 4.40
Fast break secondary option.
#2 may pass to #5 at the high post for a jump shot or to #1 for a jump shot or reversal.

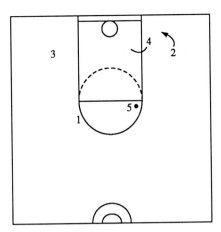

Figure 4.41
Fast break secondary option.
#5 may shoot, pass to #4 on duck-in, pass
to #2 on baseline, or pass to #3 for the
reversal and give-and-go option.

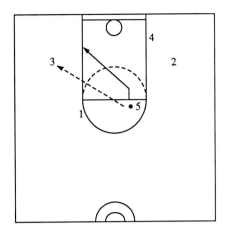

Figure 4.42
Fast break secondary option.
#5 passes to #3 and runs the give-and-go
option.

Team Defense

5

Player-to-Player Defense

Defense may not be the most enjoyable skill in the eyes of the players, but it is one phase of the game in which the team can and should be consistent. The team may have a poor shooting night but it should not have an off night on defense.

Balance and footwork are essential for good defensive play. It has often been said that you play defense from your waist down. This point is somewhat true, as proper footwork is generally considered to be most important. However, active hands can allow the defense to apply immediate pressure on the ball.

Players must understand and be able to play on-the-ball defense, denial defense, and helpside defense. Perimeter defense and post defense must work together. Players must learn to react to player movement and ball movement by shifting or jumping to their positions. A team will only be as strong as the weakest player, so it is necessary for all to understand the defense and to work as a unit.

On-the-Ball Defense

The player guarding the ball must be in position to defend the triple-threat position: the pass, the shot, and the dribble. The defensive player should be approximately an arm's distance from the offensive player. The feet are positioned with a wide base slightly more than shoulder width apart, the weight being on the balls of the feet. Unless the defensive player wishes to overplay the offense to one side, she would line up foot-to-foot with the player she is defending by putting her feet in line with the feet of the offensive player. The defender's back should be fairly straight with the knees bent and the head up. The player moves in a step-and-catch action; that is, one foot leads and the other foot catches or slides half the distance to follow. To keep the knees bent and the body low, quick or short steps are recommended over sliding the feet together.

Prior to the dribble, one of the defender's hands should be raised to defend the shot and the other extended out at waist level to protect or defend the pass. The hands should mirror the ball, or move as the ball moves, to interfere with or distract the offense. When defending the dribble, both arms are extended out to each side of the body with the hands open to the ball and the elbows bent at waist level.

Figure 5.1
On-the-ball defense.

If the offensive player shoots the ball, the defender should contest the shot by extending an open hand upward and toward the shooter, then reverse pivot to block the shooter off the boards. If the offensive player passes the ball, the defender should jump to the pass and defend the give-and-go cut. When the offensive player picks up the dribble, the defender should step close to the offensive player in a belly-up or cover-up position. The defensive player should stay between the offensive player and the basket as she mirrors the ball or covers the passing lanes and shot with active hands.

One Pass Away—Denial Defense

When the defensive player is one pass away from the ball, she should assume a denial position. This is a position that allows the defense to deny or make it more difficult for the offensive player to receive the ball. The defensive player should have her back to the ball, and the head is positioned over the shoulder on the side of the front foot to allow her to see both the ball and offensive player by using peripheral vision.

Figure 5.2
One pass away—denial defense.

The front foot and arm should be extended in the passing lane between the passer and receiver. With a proper staggered defensive stance approximately an arm's distance from the receiver and using a step-and-catch technique, the defense may deny the passing lanes as the offensive player attempts to get open. Should the offensive player receive the ball, the defender quickly steps back to an on-the-ball defensive stance between the offensive player and the basket.

If the offensive player cuts backdoor, the defense should stay in a denial until reaching the free throw lane area or until the ball is passed inside. Either situation would require the defense to reverse pivot or open to the ball (Fig. 5.2).

Two Passes Away—Helpside Defense

When the defensive player is two passes away from the ball, she assumes an open stance, or helpside position. With her back to the basket, a defensive player should be positioned in the passing lane with one hand extended toward her player and one toward the player with the ball. When the ball is on one side of the floor, the helpside defender should be in line with the rim. The farther her player is from the ball, the closer the helpside defender can be to the ball.

With helpside defense off the ball, players must be able to provide help on penetration, take a charge, defend against their player cutting to the ball, and box out their player if a shot is taken from the strong side of the court. With all of these responsibilities, the off-the-ball and helpside defenders must remain very intense, anticipate, and react to ball and player movement (Fig. 5.3).

Figure 5.3
Helpside position.

Screens on the Ball

When defending screens, the defense may use different options, such as nonswitching or switching techniques. In the nonswitching defense, the player defending the screener should recognize and verbally signal "screen." She must then step up or place her back foot next to the screener's top foot, putting herself in a position facing the player with the ball. The objective is to stop the ball, slow the offense down, or channel the offensive player away from the basket. Then the defense recovers in front of the offensive player. The defensive player that was screened should step up with her inside foot and go over the top of the screen, thus staying with her own player. Coaches should caution the defensive player on the ball not to move until the offensive player that she is guarding begins the dribble or uses the screen.

In the switching defense, the player defending the screener verbally calls the screen, and a "switch" is signaled. At this time the two defenders switch players and establish proper defensive position on each offensive player.

Screens off the Ball

Players should try to avoid getting screened when they are off the ball. When they are in an open stance, they should see the screener approaching and anticipate by stepping through or behind the screen, then recover to their player in a straight line to the passing lane.

Defending the Post

This is one of the most challenging aspects of the halfcourt defense, since many teams try to get the ball inside to score. When defending the post player, three types of defenses may be used: the defense may deny, play in front, or play behind.

Denial

The denial position is similar to the one-pass-away technique. The defense plays to one side—the ballside. The defender positions in a wide base with one foot in front and one behind the offensive player and the arms extended likewise. The head is positioned to see both the ball and the player being guarded. If the ball is passed to the opposite side, the defensive post player should step in front and then step to the side to assume the denial position again on ballside.

Playing in Front

The fronting technique is used when the defender plays in front of her offensive player and forces or encourages the lob pass. The defender should have her body in the passing lane with arms extended upwards.

Playing Behind

The third technique is used when the defensive player plays behind the post. The defender allows the post player to receive the ball and then plays the offense straight up by staying between the post player and the basket and defending the triple-threat options.

Team Concept

Once all fundamentals have been taught and rehearsed, the pieces should fit together in the player-to-player defense. Illustrations are presented to show the on-the-ball, one-pass-away, two-passes-away, and post defenses. In the diagrams, the defenders are denoted by an "A,B,C,D,E" and correspond to the specific player they are guarding by respective numbers.

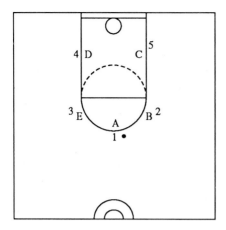

Figure 5.4
Team defense.
A1, on the ball.
B2 and E3, one pass away—denial.
C4, denial.
D5, denial.

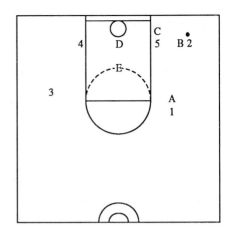

Figure 5.5
Team defense.
A1, denial on the ball.
B2. on the ball.
D4, two passes away—helpside.
E3, two passes away—helpside.
C5, one pass away—denial ballside.

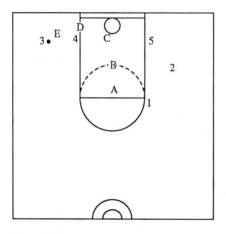

Figure 5.6
Team defense.
A1, two passes away—helpside.
B2, two passes away—helpside.
C5, two passes away—helpside.
E3, on the ball.
D4, one pass away—denial ballside.

Zone Defense

A zone defense may be used as a primary defense or as a change from the player-to-player defense. Using a zone defense (1) allows taller players to play close to the basket, providing a rebounding advantage; (2) forces perimeter shots; (3) stops one-on-one play or penetration; or (4) protects players in foul trouble. Some coaches would argue that zone defense is less difficult to teach and learn than player-to-player defense. In addition, less skilled players may be more successful within a zone defense because they have less area to defend.

There are various types of alignments that may be employed in a zone defense. One of the oldest zone defenses is the 2-3 zone, but coaches today often use the 1-2-2, 1-3-1, and match-up zone defenses.

Combination defenses are defenses that allow some players to play player-to-player and others to play zone. Such defenses include the box-and-one and the diamond-and-one. While four players set up in a box or diamond formation, one player guards an assigned person in a player-to-player defense. A triangle-and-two defense is another combination defense, with three players aligned in a triangle while two players are assigned to defend two specific offensive players.

Varying degrees of ball pressure may be used in zone defenses. Some coaches prefer to pressure the ball, whereas others apply pressure in the passing lanes or pack in the zone to force perimeter shots. Coaches should determine their preference beforehand and explain it to the team. Taller players should be positioned near the basket to provide the best possible rebounding coverage.

Although player-to-player fundamentals and principles may be used within a zone defense, general rules that are specific to zone defenses may be followed.

General Guidelines

1. Be open to the ball, with arms extended in the passing lane.
2. Defend against penetration to the middle.
3. Stop penetration on the baseline.
4. Anticipate passes and shift the zone while the ball is in the air.
5. Communicate player movement and ball movement.
6. Determine whether to front the low post or play behind.
7. Provide help from the helpside when the ball is passed inside to the post (front), and provide help from the outside when the ball is passed inside to the post (behind).

2-3 Zone Defense

The 2-3 defense is one of the most commonly used zone defenses. The guards play the top of the zone; the post, the middle, and the wings play on each baseline.

The following diagrams illustrate the different alignments of the 2-3 defense in relation to the position of the ball. The offensive players are numbered, whereas the defensive players are represented by letters of the alphabet.

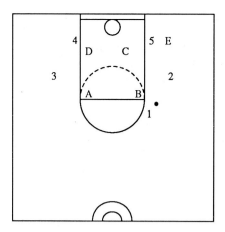

Figure 5.7
Zone defense alignment—ball on top.

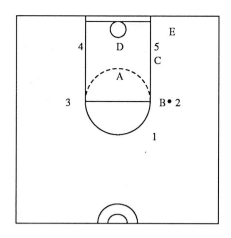

Figure 5.8
Zone defense alignment—ball at wing.

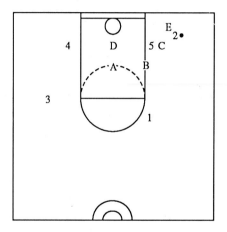

Figure 5.9
Zone defense alignment—ball in corner.

1-3-1 Zone Defense

In recent years, the 1-3-1 zone defense has been widely used. Emphasis on ball pressure and aggressive play are often used to teach the 1-3-1.

Players are assigned specific areas and must be aware of their own responsibilities. The guards are generally assigned to the top and back of the zone, and most coaches prefer to put one of their better athletes in the back of the zone. The forwards play out on the wings, while the post occupies the middle.

The player at the top of the zone should direct the ball to one side of the court. When the ball is on one of the wings, the top player rotates to the lane to help defend the middle of the lane. The player in the back of the zone begins in front of the basket. When the ball is at the wing, she plays in front of the low post. When the ball is in the corner, she plays on-the-ball defense.

The post player begins at the free throw lane. When the ball moves, the post must slide in front of any player in the lane in line with the ball. The wing player on the ball must channel the ball to the baseline. The wing player opposite the ball must cover the helpside in line with the ball.

The following illustrations will show the zone alignment when the ball is positioned at the top, on the wing, or in the corner.

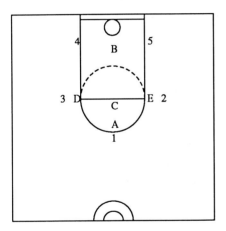

Figure 5.10
1-3-1 zone defense alignment—ball on top.

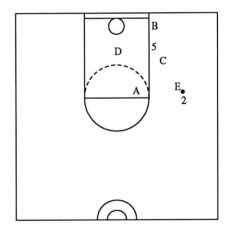

Figure 5.11
1-3-1 zone defense alignment—ball at wing.

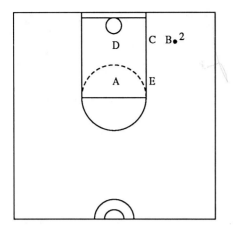

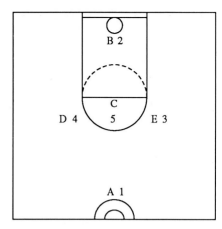

Figure 5.12
1-3-1 zone defense alignment—ball in corner.

Figure 5.13
1-3-1 halfcourt press alignment.

Transition Defense

With the tempo of today's game, it is necessary to prepare a team to defend against the fast break offense. Defensive transition requires a team to quickly convert from offense to defense. The defensive team succeeds by creating a turnover or forcing the opposition to set a halfcourt offense.

Players must learn to react and use straight-line sprints to the other end of the floor as they turn their heads to locate the ball. A defensive player may be designated to stop or influence the player with the ball by forcing the ball handler to slow down or channel her to one side of the court, while the defender's teammates retreat to the free throw lane to protect the basket. Once the ball has been stopped, the defensive players must quickly find the open or assigned player. If playing a zone, they must go to their designated area.

General Guidelines

1. Sprint and see the ball.
2. Stop the ball.
3. Influence the ball.
4. Set halfcourt defense.

Pressing Defenses

Pressing defenses are designed to allow the defense to put pressure on the offense. Traps are set to double-team the ball handler, and players off the ball are assigned to cover specific areas or passing lanes. Halfcourt and full court presses may be used when the defense is behind to force the offense to play at a faster tempo, thus creating turnovers or bad shots.

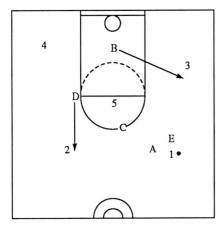

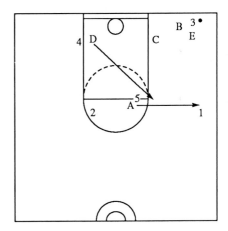

Figure 5.14

1-3-1 zone defense alignment—trap on wing.

A1 and E3 set trap on the ball.

C5 covers the high post area.

B2 covers the ballside wing and baseline.

D4 protects the basket and anticipates guard-to-guard pass.

Figure 5.15

1-3-1 zone defense alignment—trap in corner.

B & E Set trap on ball

A Covers the pass out to the ballside wing

D Covers the high post area

C Covers the low post area

1-3-1 Halfcourt Press

The 1-3-1 zone defense should be set before the offense crosses halfcourt (Fig. 5.13). Traps may either be set on the wing or in the corner.

When trapping on the wing, the top player of the zone (A) will play defense on the ball and force the ball handler to one side of the floor. At that time, the ballside wing (E) will come up and form a trap on the ball with the top player of the zone (A). The middle player (C) will cover the high post area, and the back player (B) will cover the ballside wing and baseline. The wing player opposite the trap (D) will protect the basket and anticipate the crosscourt pass (Fig. 5.14).

If the ball is passed to the corner, the ballside wing player (E) and the back player (B) may set a trap in the corner. The middle player (C) will cover the low post passing lane, the opposite wing (D) will cover the high post passing lane, and the top player (A) will cover the out pass or the ballside wing (Fig. 5.15).

Once the ball is successfully passed out of a trap, the defensive players should return to their designated areas of coverage. Quick reaction and anticipation will prevent easy baskets and allow the defense to recover.

2-2-1 Full Court Press

To get full court defenses set, it is best to press after a made basket or free throw situation. The 2-2-1 alignment begins with the guards (A and B) setting up at the free throw lane, the forwards (D and E) beginning near halfcourt, and the post (C) setting up beyond center court (Fig. 5.16).

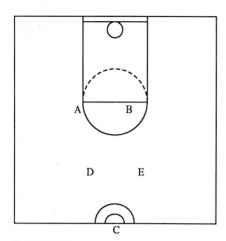

Figure 5.16
Basic 2-2-1 full court press alignment.

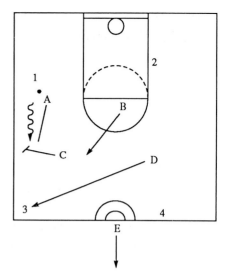

Figure 5.17
2-2-1 full court press alignment.
A1 and C3 set a trap.
B2 covers the middle of the court.
D4 covers the sideline.
E5 covers the basket.

Once the ball is passed inbounds, the guard on the ballside will influence the dribble by adding pressure on the ball and encouraging the ball handler to go up the sideline. The guard opposite the ball will move to protect the middle of the floor or diagonal passing lane. The ballside forward will look to come up and set a trap with the guard, while the other forward will move to cover the sideline or straight-on pass. The center will cover the basket or long pass (Fig. 5.17).

Should the ball be passed out of the trap, everyone should sprint ahead of the ball.

Game Preparation

6

Practice

It has often been said, "Perfect practice makes perfect."

Practice is a vital time of preparation for a team and staff. It is a time in which fundamentals, team play, and game situations should be taught, rehearsed, and polished. The coach must be organized in order to use every minute available for practice. This involves setting specific times for each phase of practice and quickly moving from one drill to another. Practice should be intense and performed at game tempo.

Our practice sessions at Tennessee are divided into three categories: the preseason, the in-season, and the postseason. The preseason begins with the first day of practice and ends with the opening game. The in-season comprises the practices during the regular season. The postseason practices are those conducted during the play-offs or tournaments.

Because the bulk of fundamental teaching occurs during the preseason, practices then are lengthier, usually 2½ hours long. During the in-season, we devote 2 hours to practice. A typical postseason practice lasts 1½ hours. To keep a team mentally and physically sharp, it is recommended that the team take off from practice at least one day a week.

The following checklist may be used in practice preparation:

( ) Stretching
( ) Warm-ups
( ) Position work
( ) Team offense
( ) Press offense
( ) Offensive breakdown drills
( ) Fast break
( ) Shooting
( ) Free throws

( ) Team defense
( ) Pressing defense
( ) Transition defense
( ) Defensive breakdown drills
( ) Out-of-bounds plays
( ) Special situations
( ) Scrimmage
( ) Conditioning

A minimum of 10 minutes should be provided before the start of practice for stretching. Warm-up may include footwork, ball handling, passing, rebounding, and so on. Position work is a time allotted for working on both offensive- and defensive-type drills at each position (guards, forwards, centers). Drills should be designed to involve as many players as possible to avoid long lines and standing around.

At Tennessee, we prefer to work no longer than 10 to 15 minutes on any one particular phase of practice. This may help to keep the players' attention. A minimum of four water breaks are taken, which last approximately 2 minutes each. Water should be readily available to the players.

The percentage of time spent on offense and defense will vary depending on the philosophy of the coach and the strength of a team. At least three days a week, we spend 50% of our time on offense and 50% on defense. Occasionally, we will go 70% on whichever aspect we think we need the most work on. We prefer to devote a minimum of 20 minutes during each practice to full court or scrimmage situations.

Sample Preseason Practice

12:30	Warm-ups
	Partner passing
	4-corner passing
	Outlet drill
	3-lane drill
12:40	Fast break
	3 on 0, 4 on 0, 5 on 0
	3 on 2, 2 on 1
	5 on 3 continuous
12:55	Transition defense
	Change drill
	Catch-up drill
1:07	Transition shooting drills
	Free throws
1:17	Water break
1:20	Offense:
	Position work
	Breakdown drills
1:30	Team offense
	Shell drill
	Halfcourt versus defense
1:38	Water break
1:40	Full court scrimmage
1:50	Shooting by positions/free throws
2:00	Water break
2:05	Defense:
	Breakdown drills
2:15	Team defense
2:35	Full court press
	Press offense
2:43	Water break
2:45	Scrimmage
2:55	Free throws
	Stretching

Once the team has mastered the Xs and Os, it's game time. Aside from practice preparation, the coach may also have scouted the opponent; thought through game preparations, time-outs, special situations, and out-of-bounds plays; and decided when to use the three-point shot. That is a lot to consider, but if the coach is prepared ahead of time, snap decisions will be made a little more comfortably.

Scouting

Scouting an upcoming opponent is commonplace on all levels of play. Whether it involves leaning against the gym wall scrutinizing the winning team in a pickup game, coaches sharing information over the phone, or professional scouting services and videotapes that cost hundreds of dollars, everyone wants to avoid fear of the unknown by scouting the opposition.

Most coaches scout opponents to better prepare their own teams in the execution of their game. The opponent's personnel may be analyzed to determine the best players as well as the weaker players. Game statistics, usually in box-score form, and overall season statistics are great sources of information about opponents. By reviewing the data, a coach can determine who the weaker free throw shooters are and who should be fouled in a close game. The statistics also point out the stronger players or the ones who shouldn't be fouled late in the game. Such information allows a team to prepare a defense against the best offensive players, take advantage of the other team's weaker defensive players, and exploit poor ball handlers.

Scouting can help a team to prepare for offensive and defensive tendencies: Does the opponent like to run or play a halfcourt game? Is it a perimeter- or post-oriented team? What is the team's best defense? Does it switch defenses? If so, when does it change? What is the most effective defense to run against this team?

Often, a team will gain confidence through a scouting report. Such information helps team members to know what to expect. Still, it is important not to place too much emphasis on what the opponents are likely to do, because not every aspect of the game can be predicted or controlled.

Game Situations

It is the coach's responsibility to prepare the team for all possible situations that may occur during the course of a game. Time should be devoted in practice to discussing and rehearsing for these possibilities.

The following checklist can serve as a guide for game preparation:

( ) Jump ball   ( ) Substitutions
( ) Offenses   ( ) Free throw situations
( ) Fast break   ( ) Shot clock
( ) Press offenses   ( ) Three-point shot
( ) Defenses   ( ) Special situations
( ) Press defenses   ( ) Rules
( ) Transition defenses   ( ) Scouting report
( ) Out-of-bounds   ( ) Time-outs
( ) Pregame meals   ( ) Bench seating
( ) Individual goals   ( ) Team goals

Time-Outs

With only five 90-second time-outs allotted per game, it is important to carefully plan and use each one wisely. Of course, the score and momentum of a game will influence when a time-out should be called, but it is generally wise to have two or three left down the stretch.

Instructions should be provided by the coach in advance to determine the floor captain or player responsible for signaling a time-out in the event that a coach cannot do so. Player-coach communication is important in being able to quickly call a necessary time-out.

Special Situations

Teams should be prepared to play the last few seconds behind, ahead, or in a tie-game situation. Last-minute scoring options should include full court and half-court strategies for all of these situations.

When the offensive team is ahead, it should be prepared to delay or stall shot attempts by using a specific halfcourt attack. Should the score be tied, a team must practice last-second scoring options with proper timing and execution. If a team is behind, pressing defenses should be rehearsed in advance.

Practice sessions need to be structured to be as game-like as possible (using officials, clocks, time-outs, and so on). The element of surprise or panic can be eliminated by practicing for special situations in advance. Drilling for these situations should be one of the most important elements in the controlled practice setting.

Shot Clock

The use of a shot clock requires the offensive team with the ball to attempt a shot at the basket within a designated time after gaining possession.

At the collegiate level, the shot clock has been a controversial issue. The NBA uses a 24-second clock, the international game has a 30-second clock, and high schools vary. Presently, the women's intercollegiate game uses a 30-second clock; the men play with a 45-second clock. Depending on the individual state high school basketball federation, some high schools are experimenting with a shot clock.

A team should use a shot clock in practice to be aware of the length of time players have to run their offense and try to get a high-percentage shot. Although the clock prevents a team from holding the ball, a team may choose to delay its offense if it wants to use time off of the shot clock.

Jump Ball

Recent rule changes at the high school and collegiate levels have eliminated most jump ball situations. A game is started by a jump ball at the center circle, and after one team gains possession, alternate possession is used in any tie-ups or jump ball decisions.

Preparation for the center jump should be organized in an attempt to gain the first possession and first possible scoring opportunity. The tallest player or best jumper normally jumps center. This player begins by facing the offensive basket and placing one foot inside the small center jump circle prior to the toss of the ball by the official. Three teammates should be positioned around the circle to help secure the ball, and one player should line up away from the circle near the opponent's basket to protect a lay-up should the opponent control the opening tip.

A quick scoring opportunity may occur from the jump ball. If not, a team must be prepared to set its halfcourt offense. The following illustrations present options that may allow a team to score off the jump ball.

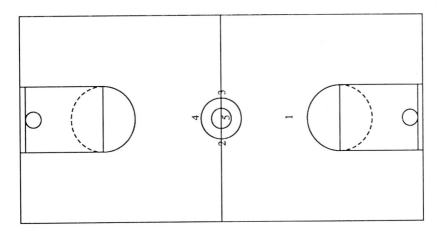

Figure 6.1
Jump ball—basic alignment.
On the toss, #5 may tip to any of the three players around the circle.

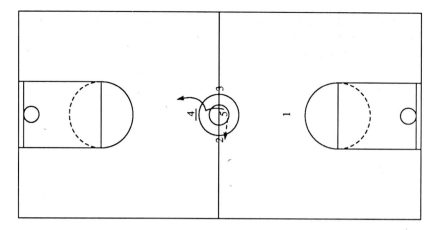

Figure 6.2
Jump ball—continuity.
If #5 tips the ball to either #2 or #3, player #4 may screen for player #5, who immediately goes to the basket.

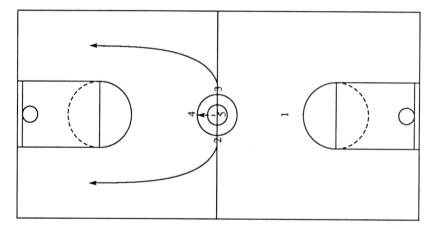

Figure 6.3
Jump ball—tip to the #4 player.
If #5 tips the ball to player #4, players #2 and #3 break to the basket on their respective wings as player #4 pivots toward the basket and looks for a high-percentage shot from either #2 or #3.

Knowledge of the rules is important so that players know when they can move into or away from the circle. Refer to game rules before instructing jump ball situations.

Out-of-Bounds Play

Set plays should be run when a team has the ball underneath its offensive basket in order to provide an opportunity for a quick or high-percentage shot. Players should be positioned carefully and given specific responsibilities.

Although most teams play a zone defense in this situation, plays should be structured to execute against either a player-to-player or a zone defense. The stack set provides several scoring options.

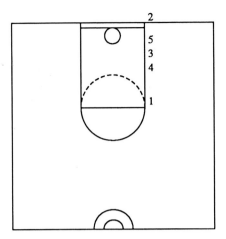

Figure 6.4
Out-of-bounds alignment.
#2—best outside shooter.

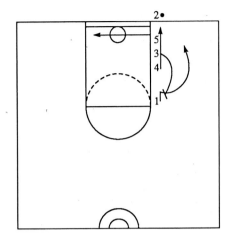

Figure 6.5
Out-of-bounds stack options.
#5 cuts in front of the defense for a possible lay-up.
#3 screen for #1, then goes to the high post.
#4 cuts straight to the ball for a possible pass.
#1 cuts to the corner for a shot or pass inside to #4.

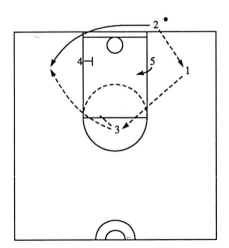

Figure 6.6
Out-of-bounds—continuity.
If shot is not taken by #4, #5, or #1:
#1 passes to #3;
#2 cuts off the screen set by #4;
#3 looks for #5 inside and #2 on the wing.

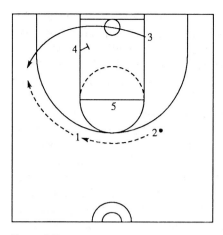

Figure 6.7
Three-point shot—screen off the ball
reversal.

Three-Point Shot

The three-point shot has added a new and exciting dimension to the game. The distance of the three-point basket varies at different levels of play. College and high school players attempt the shot from 19 feet 9 inches; the pros are several feet further back at 23 feet 9 inches.

Although this is a popular shot for spectators and players, it is not necessarily a good shot for every player. Only the best and most accurate perimeter shooters should attempt this long-range shot.

Many teams use the three-point shot as a primary attack in their halfcourt offense, some use it frequently in their fast break attack, and others use it in special situations. Its use, of course, depends on the philosophy of the coach and the personnel of the team.

Strategy for the three-point shot may include: (1) dribble or pass penetration toward the basket to draw the defense in, then a pass out to the open player stationed behind the three-point line; (2) a quick reversal or a skip pass from one side of the court to the other; (3) a screen on the ball set on or near the three-point circle to screen the defense and allow the three-point shot attempt by the ball handler; or (4) a screen off the ball, which is normally most effective when the ball is reversed or skipped from one side of the court to the other (Fig. 6.7).

Team Chemistry

In all my years of coaching, I've stood by one particular phrase when it comes to giving advice to my basketball teams: "You never have a second chance to make a first impression." I'm not sure who first uttered those words, but the phrase has always stuck in my mind, and I have repeated it in the first team meeting of the year with every team I have ever coached.

Think about it again: "You never have a second chance to make a first impression." The first impression that you leave with people will probably always stay with them. Whether it's dirty play, mouthing off to officials, or slamming the ball to the floor in disgust, or, in contrast, being polite, lending a hand to an opponent after a foul, or promptly raising your hand on a foul, people generally remember their first impressions.

Some television basketball commentators have used the phrase "all airport team," which refers to a team that looks good walking through the airport en route to a game but probably is not very talented. It's important to look good anytime that a team travels, no matter what the level of play. You never know who might see you, from the university president to the high school principal.

It is hard to be a good sport and to play within the concept of the team. Most players view their abilities and character as being more upstanding than they sometimes really are. In such cases, it is up to the coach to remind each player that there is no "I" in the word "team." Coaches should begin on the first day of practice to instill the ideal of the team concept. One of the team concept rallying points is the election or selection of team captains.

There is no hard and fast rule about selecting a captain. Some coaches prefer to have game captains so that a number of players can get the opportunity to have the responsibility of being a captain. Other coaches prefer to elect captains for the season at the beginning of the year. Electing players for each game helps to spread leadership throughout the team. Often, through this process, younger players emerge as leaders probably years sooner than if the coach had waited until they were juniors or seniors to elect them as captains.

The captain should set a good example both on and off the court. On the playing floor, the captain is an extension of the coach to the officials. In today's game, in which fighting has become more widespread, the captain is viewed by the game officials as a very important person. According to collegiate rules, the captain is the only person who may question the officials on rule interpretations or general information.

Coaches should take some time to analyze the chemistry of their team. Are there natural leaders? Do personalities mesh, or are there likely to be conflicts? Can you single out one or two players as captains? Is your team young? Do you need one person for the team members to look up to? Do you have a dress code? What is your drug or alcohol policy? Usually, school administrators pass along many of the answers. It is your responsibility to enforce them.

Rules of the Game

7

The national associations that govern basketball rules in the United States are constantly changing the rules to make the game more exciting to watch. In the last five years, a number of additions have been made to the game, including a shot clock, a three-point shot line, coaches boxes, and changes in the size of the basketball for women.

Rules are standardized on both the collegiate and high school levels. In a few instances, conferences on the collegiate level and states on the high school level have been allowed to experiment with some rule changes before these have been adopted nationwide. Currently, most high schools do not play with a shot clock, and coaches cannot stand during the game in a number of states.

Intercollegiately, the National Collegiate Athletic Association (NCAA) and the National Association of Intercollegiate Athletics (NAIA) have rules committees made up of coaches that are responsible for rule changes and modifications.

Most of the rules are basic to any level of play. The rules explained in this text represent some of the general guidelines for play.

Court Dimensions and Equipment

The size of the court is 94 feet long and 50 feet wide for collegiate and professional basketball; the high school length is reduced by 10 feet, making the dimensions 84 feet long by 50 feet wide. The three-point goal line is drawn as a semicircle 19 feet 9 inches from the basket (See Figs. 7.1 and 7.2).[1]

At the collegiate level, the backboard must be a transparent 6-foot horizontal by 4-foot vertical board with a 24-by-18-inch white rectangle centered behind a goal. The backboard is also required to have 2-inch-thick gray padding across the bottom and up the sides for protection to the players. Attached to the backboard is an 18-inch (inside diameter) bright orange ring that is parallel to the floor at a height of 10 feet.

The ball for men should be 29½ to 30 inches in circumference and weigh no more than 20 to 22 ounces. The ball for women is slightly smaller, with a circumference of 28½ to 29 inches and a weight of 18 to 20 ounces. Both balls are leather-covered and should be of the molded variety.

1. *1989 NCAA Illustrated Basketball, Men's and Women's Rules* (Shawnee Mission, Kans.: NCAA Publishing Service, 1988): 16–17.

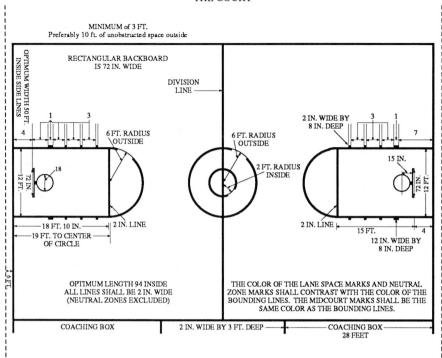

Source: Dr. Edward S. Steitz, Editor NCAA Basketball Rules

Figure 7.1
Basketball court dimensions. Source: Dr. Edward S. Steitz, Editor NCAA Basketball Rules.

A recent rule for intercollegiate basketball is the establishment of a 28-foot coaching box. Coaches are required to stay in the coaching box during the game or they will be assessed with a technical foul. Many states have adopted a rule that coaches may not stand up while coaching a high school game. These rule changes have come as a result of poor bench decorum.

Players, Substitutes, and Jerseys

A basketball team consists of five players plus substitutes. The names of all players who could possibly play must be entered into the scorebook prior to the start of the game. Only the players whose names and jersey number appear in the book may play. At least one player is designated as the captain, and this player represents the team and coaches to the game officials.

To enter the game, a substitute must report to the official scorer and announce his or her name and number and the name and number of the player being replaced. Substitutes can enter the game only when the clock stops on a sounded horn, the ball is dead, and the official motions the player to enter the game.

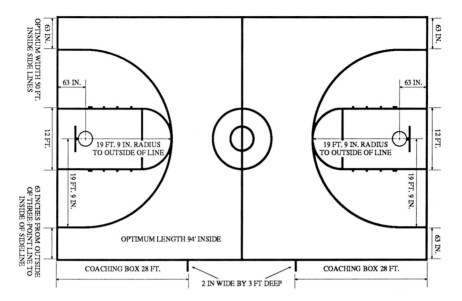

Figure 7.2
Court dimensions for three-point shot. Source: Dr. Edward S. Steitz, Editor NCAA Basketball Rules.

Game jerseys must be alike and have numbers on both the front and the back. The back numbers should be at least 6 inches high; the numbers on the front need to be 4 inches high. Numbers 1 and 2 and any single digit greater than 5 are illegal. Legal numbers start with double-zero, 3, 4, and 5 (single digits) and then in fives (10–15, 20–25, 30–35, 40–45, 50–55).

Several years ago, a popular practice was to wear a t-shirt under the jersey. It may still be worn but must be of the same color as the game jersey. Also, at no time may a player wear jewelry on the court. Violation of either of these rules results in a technical foul.

Scoring, Timing, and the Shot Clock

There are three ways that points are scored in a basketball game. A field goal is scored when a live ball passes down through the basket. Two points are awarded to the team whose basket the ball passed through. A goal is scored even if a player accidentally scores at the wrong basket; in such a case, points are credited to the opponent. Three points are awarded for shots taken from behind the three-point line. The official signals the goal with arms straight over the head and three fingers held up. A free throw (a shot taken as a result of fouls or rules infractions) is credited with one point.

The length of the game varies at different levels of play:

Colleges play two 20-minute halves with a 15-minute intermission between the halves.

High schools play four 8-minute quarters with a 10-minute halftime and 1-minute breaks after the first and third quarters.

Youth leagues and grade schools play 6- or 7-minute quarters with breaks similar to the high schools.

At the end of regulation time, if the score is tied, a 5-minute overtime will be played. Fouls remain the same, but each team is awarded an extra time-out in addition to any time-outs left from regulation play. These 5-minute overtimes will be played until a winner is determined.

A period ends when time has expired. However, if a ball is in flight on a field goal attempt or a foul is called as time expires, the field goal will count if it is good and the free throws will be awarded to the player who was fouled.

Each team receives five time-outs per game and one extra time-out for each overtime period. Any other called time-outs past the allotted five will result in a technical foul.

After the initial center jump ball by one player from each team to start the game, the clock runs. The clock is only stopped when a time-out or foul is called, the ball goes out of bounds, or an infraction of the rules whistles the play dead.

Several years ago, coaches would sometimes get a lead and then "freeze the ball" or go into a stall until the final buzzer. Now a shot clock dictates that the offense must get a shot off in 45 seconds in men's basketball, 30 seconds in women's basketball, and 24 seconds in professional basketball. The clock is reset when the team in control of the ball attempts a field goal, possession changes, or there is a dead-ball situation.

Rule Definitions

Alternating possession has taken the place of jump balls after the initial jump ball to start the game. The team that does not control the tip to start the game will be awarded the ball on the next jump ball situation.

The **basket** is the 18-inch orange ring that players attempt to shoot the ball into.

Basket interference occurs when an offensive player interferes with the ball or basket when the ball is in the imaginary cylinder above the basket, within the basket, or live on the rim. On a two-point shot, two points are awarded, on a three-point shot, three points are awarded, and on a free throw try, one point is awarded. The player whose shot was interfered with receives credit for the goal.

Blocking is called when one player impedes the progress or makes contact with a player who does not have the ball.

Bonus free throws are awarded after the successful completion of the front-end (first) free throw in a one-and-one situation.

Control is established when a player is passing or dribbling the ball. **Team control** occurs when two players pass the ball.

Disqualified players are players who have committed their fifth foul, thus fouling out of the game, or players ejected from the game.

A **dribble** is a movement of the ball resulting when a player bounces it against the floor and continues to bounce the ball without picking it up. The ball can be hit with either hand but not both at the same time. The dribble ends when the ball is picked up or struck with both hands. The violation is called a double dribble.

A **foul** is an infraction of the rules. These include common, double, intentional, multiple, personal, or player control fouls. In a bonus situation, the foul is awarded with a free throw in the case of the seventh foul called in a half. More severe fouls, such as flagrant, technical, and unsportsmanlike fouls, result in automatic free throws.

A **free throw** is an undisturbed try for a one-point goal from a line 15 feet from the basket.

Frontcourt and **backcourt** are the areas of the floor on either side of the division or halfcourt line. A team's front court is the area where its basket is located, and the backcourt is the remainder of the court containing the opponent's basket.

Goaltending occurs when an offensive player interferes with the ball or basket on a field goal or free throw try. Points are awarded (three for a three-point goal, two for a two-point goal, and one on a free throw) if the official determines basket interference.

A **jump ball** is the play that begins the game and all overtime periods.

Traveling is called when a player moves with the ball without dribbling, sometimes called taking "steps."

A **violation** is an infraction less serious than a foul.

Violations and Penalties

Violations can come in many forms in the game of basketball. Floor violations usually result in the ball being given to the opposing team out of bounds nearest where the violation occurred. Other violations include goaltending (for which one, two, or three points are awarded to the opponent), free throw violations, and fouls (the most serious of violations).

Common Violations

1. Traveling (walking) with the ball, kicking it, or striking it with the fist.
2. Throwing the ball into the basket from the bottom to the top.
3. Stopping a continuous dribble and then dribbling again (double dribble).
4. Not advancing the ball from the backcourt in 10 seconds.
5. Goaltending or basket interference.
6. Standing in the lane more than 3 seconds on offense.
7. Failing to attempt a field goal before the shot clock expires.
8. Stepping into the lane too quickly on a free throw.
9. Stepping over the line while attempting a free throw.
10. Faking a free throw on purpose.

Fouls

More serious infractions are fouls. Each player gets five fouls per game in inter-collegiate basketball, and technical fouls do not count in this total. Fouls are classified either as personal or technical.

Personal Fouls

Free throws are awarded in a bonus situation (after the seventh team foul of each half). Players shoot the first free throw, and, if they are successful, they are given a second free throw attempt. If the bonus situation is not in effect, the offended team is awarded the ball out of bounds.

If the personal foul occurs during a made basket, one free throw is awarded. If the shooter is fouled in the act of shooting, she is awarded two free throw attempts.

Flagrant and intentional fouls are the most serious of all. Teams not only get to shoot two free throws, but they also get possession of the ball out of bounds.

The rules have become very strict on fighting. Currently, any player involved in fighting is on probation the first time; is given a one-game suspension and ejected from the game the second time; and is suspended from all competition (including tournaments) for the remainder of the year the third time.

Technical Fouls

Technical fouls are assessed for a variety of reasons. Among these are the following: failing to turn in a starting line-up 10 minutes before tip-off; taking excessive time-outs; having more than five players on the floor; have an illegal number; wearing jewelry; delaying the game; slapping the backboard; grabbing or hanging from the rim; unnecessary roughness when giving the ball to the official; reporting into the game without checking in with the official scorers; flagrant use of profanity; a coach leaving the coaching box; and not replacing a fouled-out player within 30 seconds.

Major Differences between Men's and Women's Basketball Rules

Years ago, there was a great deal of difference between men's and women's basketball rules on the collegiate level. Today, differences still exist, but the game is becoming more similar as the rules continue to evolve to make the game both safer and more exciting.

The differences in the rules range from fouls to violations to time-outs to the number of the officials on the court. There are about nine major rules differences currently found in the game:

1. Men have 10 seconds to get the ball from the backcourt to the frontcourt. There is no 10-second count in women's basketball.
2. The shot clock in women's basketball is set for 30 seconds; in men's basketball it is set for 45 seconds.
3. In men's basketball, there are usually three officials, consisting of one referee and two umpires. In women's basketball, there are two officials—an umpire and a referee.
4. A change in the rules now assesses all bench technical fouls to the coach and awards two free throws.
5. In women's basketball, the coach or players may call a time-out. In men's basketball, only a player may request a time-out.
6. There are four marked spaces on the free throw lane and one unmarked space near the free throw line. In men's basketball, all of the spaces may be used; in the women's game, the fifth space must be left vacant.
7. In women's basketball, the rule regarding a "closely guarded player" applies anywhere on the court when a player is holding the ball and the defense contains that player at a distance of 3 feet for 5 seconds. In men's basketball, the violation occurs only in the frontcourt when a defensive player is guarding the player holding or dribbling the ball at a distance of 6 feet.
8. One of the most controversial fouls and differences in the game concerns the airborne shooter. In men's basketball, there is no airborne shooter rule. Essentially, if a player commits a charging foul on a field goal attempt and the basket is good, it is counted and the shooter is given a pushing foul. The "gentleman's rule" is in effect; you get the basket, but you also get charged with the foul. In women's basketball, if the defense is set prior to the shooter becoming airborne, and the shooter crashes into the defense, the basket is wiped off and the foul is called on the offensive player, or airborne shooter.
9. In the area of extra apparel, women are not permitted to wear running or biking lycra tights under their uniforms which extend below their playing shorts. Men are permitted to do so. However, neither may wear t-shirts under their jerseys that are not of the same color as their uniform top.

Glossary

Assist
A pass that leads directly to a made basket.

Backboard
The rectangular, usually fiberglass structure that supports the goal or basket.

Backcourt
The half of the court opposite a team's offensive basket.

Backdoor
A play in which an offensive player cuts behind the defense toward the basket.

Bank Shot
A shot in which the ball hits the backboard before entering the basket.

Baseball Pass
A long pass down court, used primarily on the fast break.

Basket
A metal ring (18 inches in diameter) that is positioned in the center of the backboard to which a net is attached and suspended.

Baseline
End line or boundary line of the court that runs behind each basket.

Blocked Shot
A situation that occurs when a defensive player legally touches a ball being shot by an offensive player, resulting in a missed basket.

Blocking Out
A technique used by the defense to prevent the offensive player from getting position to get a rebound.

Bounce Pass
A pass made when the player with the ball bounces the ball off the floor to a teammate. Used most frequently on the fast break or to pass to post players.

Box-and-One
Combination defense in which one player plays player-to-player defense while four players play a zone in a box formation.

Center
A player that plays nearest the basket.

Change of Pace
Term used to describe a player changing speed—for example, from fast to slow to fast.

Charging

What occurs when an offensive player runs into a defensive player who has established position.

Chest Pass

A pass made from chest level; the most fundamental pass in basketball.

Clear Out

To move players out of a certain area of the court to allow a single player to go one-on-one.

Controlling the Boards

Refers to a team that dominates the rebounding.

Crossover Dribble

A technique in which the player with the ball dribbles or bounces the ball with one hand across the body and changes the ball to the other hand.

Cut

A sharp change of direction normally made by an offensive player to get free of the defense in order to receive the ball.

Dead

The term verbally signaled on defense when the offense picks up its dribble.

Defensive Rebound

A rebound retrieved by a defensive player.

Denial

A defensive position assumed to keep the offensive player from receiving the ball.

Double Dribble

A violation that occurs when a player stops dribbling, picks up the ball, and then begins to dribble again.

Double Post

Offensive strategy of using two post players—either two low posts or a high and a low post.

Double-Team

What happens when two defensive players guard one offensive player.

Drive

An offensive move toward the basket.

Duck In

A cut or movement by an offensive player who is away from the ball into the low post area toward the ball.

Dunking

The action of an offensive player who goes over the rim and pushes or throws the ball down through the basket.

Elbow

An area at the high post; specifically, where the corners of the free throw lines meet.

Fake Pass

A situation in which the player with the ball fakes a pass to get the defense to react.

Fast Break

When a team quickly breaks to its offensive basket from the defensive end.

Filling the Lanes

Refers to the lanes filled by players on the fast break.

Flash

A movement or cut by an offensive player who is away from the ball into a passing lane toward the ball.

Forward

Normally, the player who plays the wing or baseline position.

Forward Pivot

The action taken when with one foot stationary on the floor, a player steps forward or in a circular pattern using her other foot.

Foul

Illegal contact that is an infraction of the rules.

Free Lance

Offense designed for players to have freedom to use their skills rather than a structured offense.

Free Throw

A 15-foot unguarded shot taken at the free throw line as a result of a foul.

Fronting the Post

Refers to the defensive guarding position when the defense gets in front of the post player.

Frontcourt

The half of the court in which the offensive team's basket is located.

Give-and-Go

Offensive strategy in which a player passes the ball and immediately cuts toward the basket, looking for a pass.

Goaltending

A violation that occurs when a player interferes with the ball or basket once the ball is in a downward flight to the basket.

Guard

Normally the smaller player that plays the point guard or a wing position.

Helpside Defense

Defense that is on the opposite side of the court from the ball; also called weakside defense.

High Post

The area of the court across the free throw line—also used to identify a post player playing in that area.

Hook Shot

A shot that is usually taken close to the basket in which a player shoots the ball from one shoulder over her head to the basket.

Jump Ball

Action used to begin the game in which two opposing players jump to tip the ball thrown straight up in the air by the referee at center court.

Jump Shot

A shot at the basket taken by an offensive player as the player stops, jumps up, and releases the ball near the peak of the jump.

Jump Stop

A stop executed when a player lands on both feet simultaneously.

Key

Free throw lane and circle area above the free throw line.

Lay-Up

A shot that is taken close to the basket, normally by a player driving to the basket.

Low Post

Area of the court near the basket in the free throw lane area; also used to identify the post player playing in that area.

Offensive Rebounding

A rebound retrieved by an offensive player.

On the Line

Position that a defensive player off the ball assumes by playing in the passing lanes between her player and the ball.

One-on-One

Term used to describe one player going against another player.

Outlet Pass

A pass made by a player to initiate the change from defense to offense, most commonly used after a defensive rebound.

Overtime

Extra time allotment used to determine a winner when the score is tied at the end of regulation time.

Pass and Cut

Offensive strategy in which a player passes the ball and immediately cuts, looking for a return pass.

Pivot

Refers to a footwork fundamental in which one foot remains stationary on the floor.

Player-to-Player

Term used on defense to describe each defensive player guarding one offensive player (also called man-to-man).

Post

Normally, the taller player or players on the team who play near the basket in the free throw lane area.

Pressing Defense

Defense used to specifically pressure the ball or passing lanes.

Rebound

What occurs when a player gains possession of the ball on a missed shot as it comes off the backboard or rim.

Reverse Pivot

The action taken when with one foot stationary on the floor, a player steps backwards and pivots in a circular pattern.

Sagging Defense

The position a defensive player assumes when she drops off or backs away from her own player.

Screen

An offensive tactic in which a player establishes a stationary position and blocks a defensive player; also called a pick.

Screen and Roll

A two-player offensive maneuver in which the player with or without the ball screens for a player with the ball. The screener rolls to the basket as the ball is dribbled around the screen.

Single Post

Refers to a team offense using only one post player.

Skip Pass

A pass used to swing or reverse the ball from one side of the court to the other.

Split the Post

Three-player offensive maneuver in which a pass is thrown to a high post and two players cut by the high post.

Stall

What occurs when the offensive team holds the ball or uses as much time on the shot clock as possible before attempting a shot.

Steal

What happens when a defensive player legally gains possession of the ball from an offensive player.

Switch

What happens when a defensive player changes or switches the player she is guarding with another teammate.

Three-Second Lane

The area of the court from the free throw line to the baseline within the free throw lane area.

Tip-In

Action occurring when a player tips or taps the ball in on a missed shot.

Top of Key

Circular area above the free throw lane.

Trailer

The offensive player on the fast break who follows the ball down the floor and to the ballside low post.

Traveling

Violation that occurs when a player with the ball takes too many steps without dribbling.

Triple-Threat Position

The position of the offensive player who has received the ball and is able to pass, shoot, or dribble.

Turnover

Violation by one team that awards the ball to the other team.

Two-Step Stop

Stop executed when a player lands first on one foot and then on the other.

Up the Line

Position a defensive player off the ball assumes by playing on the line and closer to the ball.

Weakside

Defense that is on the opposite side of the court from the ball; also called helpside defense.

Wing

The player that plays facing the basket in the free throw lane extended area.

Zone Defense

The type of defense in which players defend a particular area of the court instead of a specific player.

Questions and Answers

True or False

1. The game of basketball was invented by Dr. Luther Gulick.   T or F
2. Flexibility refers to the capability of a joint to function through its entire range of motion.   T or F
3. "Box out" is the term most frequently used in reference to rebounding on the defensive end of the court.   T or F
4. Good footwork is a key to good balance.   T or F
5. The triple-threat position is sometimes known as the ready position. T or F
6. The give-and-go is a three-player technique.   T or F
7. The flex offense would be particularly appropriate for a team with several good post players.   T or F
8. A player or team may have a poor defensive game once in a while but should never have a bad shooting game.   T or F
9. A defensive player who is one pass away should assume a helpside position.   T or F
10. A middle player on the fast break is the primary decision maker.   T or F
11. Cardiovascular endurance is the most important component of a basketball conditioning program.   T or F
12. Overtime always starts with a jump ball.   T or F
13. All players are allowed only 3 seconds in the free throw lane area. T or F
14. The box-and-one is referred to as a combination defense.   T or F
15. The screen and roll is a two-player technique.   T or F
16. Both the men's and women's game have a 10-second backcourt rule. T or F
17. It is not a technical foul if a player changes jersey numbers at halftime.   T or F
18. The triangle-and-two is a special offensive strategy.   T or F
19. Only the coach may call a time-out during a dead ball.   T or F
20. Only the team in possession of the ball may substitute.   T or F

Completion

1. The dimensions of a collegiate basketball floor are _____ .
2. The four major components of physical fitness for a basketball player are _____ , _____ , _____ , and _____ .
3. From the triple-threat position, a player should be ready to _____ , _____ , or _____ .
4. The most fundamental shot in basketball is the _____ .
5. The #1 player in a typical offensive set is usually called the _____ .
6. A defensive player should be in the _____ position if she is guarding a player who is one pass away.
7. The three-point circle in collegiate and high school basketball is at a distance of _____ from the basket.
8. The amount of time a team has on the shot clock in collegiate basketball is _____ for the men and _____ for the women.
9. The _____ is a technique used to change direction while keeping one foot in constant contact with the floor.
10. Each team is allowed to call _____ time-outs during a game.
11. The overtime period is _____ minutes long.
12. During an overtime, each team is awarded _____ additional time-out(s).
13. The free throw lane is _____ feet wide.
14. A shot that hit the backboard before going into the basket is called a _____ shot.
15. The _____ _____ offense may be used if a team has only one true post player.
16. The _____ pass is often used by perimeter players to get the ball inside to a post player.
17. The _____ dribble is a combination of a control and speed dribble.
18. The three techniques used to guard the post include _____ , _____ , and _____ .
19. The _____ shot is one of today's most advanced shooting techniques.
20. The _____ pass is frequently used in the fast break offense.
21. The player that plays nearest to the basket is referred to as the post player or _____ .
22. _____ defense is when each person is assigned to a specific area and a _____ defense is when each person is assigned to a player.
23. A pass used to reverse the ball from one side of the court to the other is called a _____ pass.
24. A violation by one team that rewards the ball to another is called a _____ .

Question Answer Key

True or False

1. False
2. True
3. True
4. True
5. True
6. False
7. False
8. False
9. False
10. True

11. True
12. True
13. False
14. True
15. True
16. False
17. True
18. False
19. False
20. False

Completion

1. 94 feet by 50 feet
2. Flexibility, strength, muscular endurance, cardiorespiratory endurance
3. Pass, shoot, or dribble
4. Lay-up
5. Point
6. Denial
7. 19 feet 9 inches
8. 45 and 30 seconds
9. Pivot
10. Five
11. Five
12. One
13. 12 feet
14. Bank
15. Single post
16. Bounce
17. Hesitation
18. Deny, front, behind
19. Jump
20. Baseball
21. Center
22. Zone, player-to-player
23. Skip
24. Turnover

Index